DECK CODES & STANDARDS

How to Design, Build, Inspect & Maintain a Safer Deck

Bruce A. Barker

COOL
SPRINGS
PRESS

Inspiring | Educating | Creating | Entertaining

Brimming with creative inspiration, how-to projects, and useful information to enrich your everyday life, Quarto Knows is a favorite destination for those pursuing their interests and passions. Visit our site and dig deeper with our books into your area of interest: Quarto Creates, Quarto Cooks, Quarto Homes, Quarto Lives, Quarto Drives, Quarto Explores, Quarto Gifts, or Quarto Kids.

First published in 2017 by Cool Springs Press, an imprint of The Quarto Group,
401 Second Avenue North, Suite 310, Minneapolis, MN 55401 USA.
T (612) 344-8100 F (612) 344-8692 www.QuartoKnows.com

10 9 8 7 6 5 4 3 2 1

ISBN: 978-1-59186-685-5

Acquiring Editor: Mark Johanson
Project Manager: Alyssa Bluhm
Art Director: Brad Springer
Layout: Danielle Smith-Boldt

Printed in China

NOTICE TO READERS

For safety, use caution, care, and good judgment when following the procedures described in this book. The publisher, author, and BLACK+DECKER cannot assume responsibility for any damage to property or injury to persons as a result of misuse of the information provided.

The information and techniques shown in this book are general techniques for various applications. In some instances, additional information and techniques not shown in this book may be required. Always follow manufacturers' instructions included with products, since deviating from the directions may void warranties and may cause product failure that results in injury. The projects in this book vary widely as to skill levels required: some may not be appropriate for all do-it-yourselfers, and some may require professional help.

Consult your local building department for information on building permits, codes, and other laws as they apply to your project.

Contents

Deck Codes & Standards

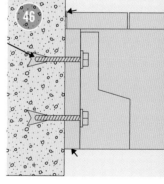

Chapter 1:
Is My Deck Safe?

Maybe your deck is safe. There is, however, a good chance that it is not safe, at least when evaluated using current codes and standards. In this chapter and in the next chapter, we discuss how you can begin assessing whether or not your deck is safe. We also discuss some common myths and rationalizations that arise when people think about their decks.

What Are the Odds?

Reliable statistics about injuries and deaths involving decks are difficult to obtain. Conservative estimates from the mid-2000s are around 4,000 per year. Other estimates from that period are as high as 35,000 per year. Some estimates place the number above 120,000. Whatever the actual number, there were, and still are, a lot of injuries and deaths involving decks, most of which are preventable.

Given these statistics, what are the odds of you, your family, or your friends being injured—or worse—while using your deck? The odds are very low. That said, it is prudent for every deck owner to determine the level of risk he or she is willing to assume.

A good way to begin assessing the risk posed by your deck is to determine its age. The risk posed by a deck increases with age. The risk profile is not linear, meaning that the risk increases at a faster rate with each year of aging. Figure 1 shows a visual representation of the relative risk posed by a deck as it ages.

Age is only one risk factor. Other risk factors include whether the deck was built under a permit with approved inspections, codes and standards in effect and enforced when the deck was built, environmental conditions (such as frequent precipitation, exposure to saltwater), deck construction materials and methods used, and deck maintenance.

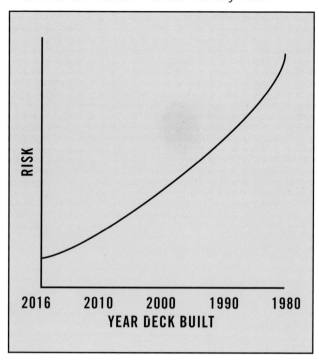

FIGURE 1: Relative Deck Safety Risk

Deck Service Life

The service life of a deck can be divided into two categories. One category is the service life of the deck components, such as the wood and the fasteners. The other category might be called functional obsolescence.

Deck component service life varies over a wide range that depends on factors including environmental conditions and maintenance. The range varies from as little as 5 to 10 years for a deck located directly on the ocean to as many as 25 years for a well-maintained deck in a dry environment, such as a desert. A common estimate for the service life of an average deck, in an average environment, with average maintenance, is between 10 and 20 years.

Functional obsolescence refers to a deck that deviates significantly from current codes and standards. The deck components may be in good condition, but a functionally obsolete deck is not safe because it lacks features that we now know are essential for safety. This book peresents many of these features. While the odds of injury are low while using a functionally obsolete deck, a functionally obsolete deck presents risks that could result in injury, or worse. It may be possible to update a functionally obsolete deck, if the deck components are intact and within their service lives. It usually makes little sense to update a deck if the components are in poor condition and past the end of their service lives.

Evolution of National Deck Codes and Standards

When a deck was built has a significant impact on whether or not it is safe. Before the 2006 edition of the International Residential Code (IRC), the IRC had very little to say about how to build a deck. Each new IRC edition since then contains more prescriptive guidance about how to build a deck. Prescriptive guidance means that if you build the deck as described in the IRC, the

deck will pass code inspection. Unfortunately, even the most recent IRC edition (2015) contains no prescriptive guidance about several important deck construction issues, such as guard post attachment and stair attachment to the deck. Lack of prescriptive guidance leaves deck builders to guess about how to comply with IRC requirements. Frequently, these guesses are not good.

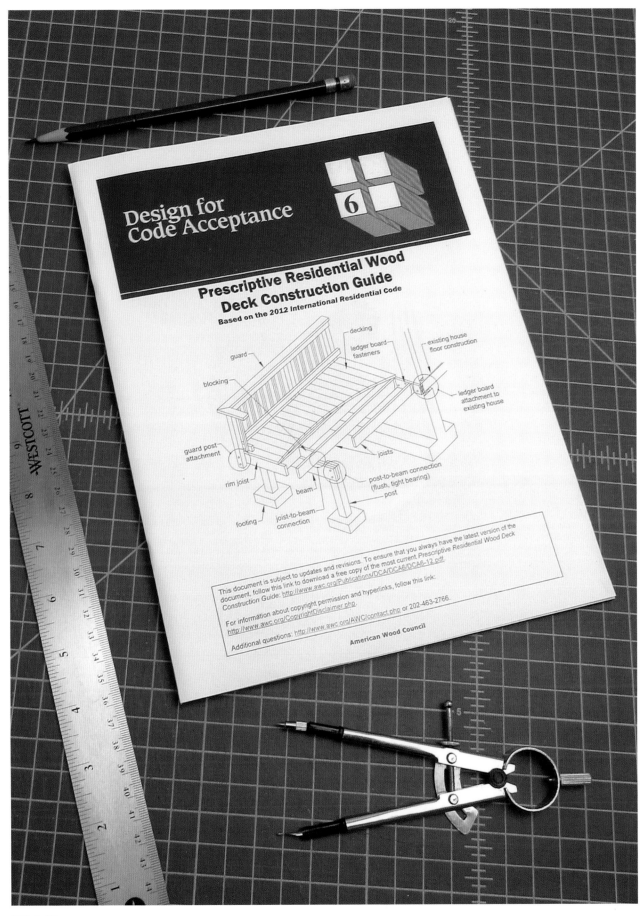

Design for Code Acceptance

6

Prescriptive Residential Wood Deck Construction Guide

Based on the 2012 International Residential Code

decking

guard

ledger board fasteners

existing house floor construction

blocking

ledger board attachment to existing house

guard post attachment

joists

rim joist

post-to-beam connection (flush, tight bearing)

beam

post

footing

joist-to-beam connection

This document is subject to updates and revisions. To ensure that you always have the latest version of the document, follow this link to download a free copy of the most current Prescriptive Residential Wood Deck Construction Guide: http://www.awc.org/Publications/DCA/DCA6/DCA6-12.pdf.

For information about copyright permission and hyperlinks, follow this link: http://www.awc.org/CopyrightDisclaimer.php.

Additional questions: http://www.awc.org/AWC/contact.php or 202-463-2766.

American Wood Council

DCA 6-12.

A significant leap forward in the evolution of deck codes and standards is *DCA 6–Prescriptive Residential Deck Construction Guide* from the American Wood Council. The first edition of this guide was based on the 2006 IRC. The current edition is DCA 6-12. It is a free PDF available to download at www.awc.org/codes-standards/publications/dca6. DCA 6 goes beyond the IRC in terms of prescriptive guidance and best practices for building decks. Everyone who builds or inspects decks should have a copy of this document. Many of the recommendations in this book come from DCA 6-12 and the IRC.

Prescriptive guidance in DCA 6 and the IRC did not just happen. This guidance is based on research conducted by Dr. Frank Woeste and Dr. Joe Loferski at Virginia Tech, and Dr. Don Bender at Washington State. Guidance based on research and testing is far more reliable than guidance based on other considerations. Reliability is an important consideration, especially when dealing with local codes and standards that differ from the DCA 6 and IRC.

Local Deck Codes and Standards

Almost all areas of the United States have adopted some version of a building code. Some states, such as California, Florida, North Carolina, and New York, have a state building code. Some large cities, such as Chicago and New York City, have a city building code. Many of these state and local building codes are based on the model codes from the International Code Council (ICC). Smaller cities and counties often use ICC model codes, such as the IRC. Some rural areas may not have adopted a building code, but this is becoming an uncommon situation.

Most building departments that use the IRC adopt local changes to the code. Many of these changes are minor and help to adapt the IRC to local conditions and needs. Some of these changes significantly alter IRC provisions. The building department should publish, in writing, any changes adopted by the local government.

Codes and standards vary between jurisdictions. This variability includes how and when codes and standards are interpreted and enforced. However, some common themes apply to most local codes and standards.

One common theme is that local adoption of codes proceeds slowly. Jurisdictions are often at least one edition behind the most current edition of the IRC. Sometimes, they are two or more editions behind. For example, if the 2015 IRC edition is the most current, your local jurisdiction could be using the 2009 IRC, or an even earlier edition. A deck built in 2016 could, therefore, be built using a much older and less effective code.

Another common theme is that codes are political documents. As is usually true in politics, some jurisdictions are more progressive and others are more conservative. Jurisdictions such as Fairfax County, Virginia, and the State of Georgia have adopted state-of-the-art deck codes. Other jurisdictions have not adopted state-of-the-art codes, or may have adopted codes that are not based on research and testing. A deck built in 2016 in a more conservative jurisdiction could, therefore, be built using a much less effective code.

My Deck Was Permitted and Inspected

A common myth is that decks that are built under a permit and have passed inspection are free from code violations and are safe. Passing an inspection means that the inspector did not find a violation of the code in effect at the time of the inspection. The deck may have code violations, and may not be safe even after passing inspection.

A deck built before the evolution of current deck codes and standards may be functionally obsolete because the code at the time provided minimal prescriptive guidance. A deck built today under a less effective code and standard may be functionally obsolete, and may not be safe, when built.

There are many good government building inspectors. They all suffer from two common limitations though. First, they are limited to enforcing the code adopted by their jurisdiction. Second, they often have limited time to perform an inspection. This time limitation can cause a less thorough inspection than the inspector would probably like to perform. These limitations can result in a less safe deck, even when the deck is built under a permit and has passed inspection.

An approved design and the issuance of a permit do not ensure that your deck is safe. Even field inspections have limitations. Ultimately, ensuring a safe deck is the responsibility of the homeowner and builder.

I Don't Need a Permit!

Actually, you do need a permit to build a deck in almost parts of the United States. You need a permit because building a deck without a permit is illegal and risky. You could be forced to remove an illegally built deck. You are required to disclose unpermitted work on most seller disclosure statements when you sell a house. If you do not disclose the unpermitted work, and if there is a problem, you could be held liable for the costs of those problems, including costs of personal injury and death.

A deck built under the worst building code in the country is better than a deck built without a permit, if for no other reason than a deck built with a permit is built legally. Building codes are a minimum standard. A minimum standard is usually better than no standard, which is what occurs when a deck is built without a permit.

You always have the option to build a deck that exceeds minimum standards. A deck built using DCA 6-12 should pass inspection in most, if not all, jurisdictions. When built under a permit, the deck is legal. A legally built deck that exceeds minimum standards is the best possible outcome.

My Deck Is Grandfathered

Grandfathering is an informal term referring to a generally true rule that existing structures are not required to be brought up to current building code requirements. Grandfathering is another myth. While this rule is generally true, there is an exception for safety. IRC Section R102.7 allows the local building official to require upgrades "for the general safety and welfare of the occupants and the public." This exception is rarely enforced, but it makes a very important point. There is no grandfathering of safety defects.

Why would you want to grandfather a safety defect? If something is unsafe now, does it matter if it was considered safe in the past? The answer is, or should be, that it does not matter. An unsafe condition should be corrected, period.

Codes change and usually for a very good reason. A deck built back in the 1990s with 8"-dia. concrete footings and 4 × 4 posts was viewed as safe at the time but it would not pass inspection today. Research, testing, and experience have taught us that more robust construction and materials are necessary to build a safe deck.

My Deck Looks Fine

Many decks look fine, from one perspective. Most people only look at the top side of their deck. Most people do not spend much, if any, time looking closely under their deck. If there are serious safety defects, this is usually where to find them. Even those who look under their deck usually do not know what to look for. If you do not know what a safety defect looks like, you will not find it. By the end of this book, you should have a better understanding of what deck safety defects look like, where to find them, and what to do about them.

The *Titanic* Sank

Some believe that pressure washing a deck and applying a wood coating can somehow make an old deck like new. This type of cosmetic refreshment will do nothing for a deck that has deteriorated components or a deck that is functionally obsolete. Cosmetic refreshment of a deck that is deteriorated or that is functionally obsolete has been compared to rearranging the deck chairs on the *Titanic*. Cosmetic refreshment can actually make the safety situation worse by providing a false sense of security.

Deck maintenance begins with using the right materials to build the deck and installing them according to best practices and the manufacturer's instructions for fasteners, connectors, and joist hangers. It continues with the application of a good quality stain or other wood coating applied according to manufacturer's instructions soon after the deck is built, and at regular intervals thereafter. This help protects the wood from deterioration caused by moisture and sunlight. It further continues with regular inspections to detect, and if necessary replace, deteriorated wood and other components. Good maintenance and regular inspections can extend the life of a deck. Cosmetic refreshment does not.

A quality exterior wood stain with UV protection will protect your wood deck and prolong its lifespan, but if the wood has begun to deteriorate a coating of stain will do nothing to help your deck.

The Overloaded Deck Myth

A deck collapses. An "expert" goes on television or is quoted in the newspaper blaming the collapse on an overloaded deck. It is possible to overload a deck with a hot tub or other very heavy object. It is very difficult to overload a properly designed and constructed deck with people. The following is what a real expert (Frank Woeste, PhD, professor emeritus, Virginia Tech University) says about the overloaded deck myth: "Most decks and guardrails collapse because they were not properly designed and constructed. It is practically impossible to overload a deck designed and built to the 40 psf live load requirement, or for a properly designed and constructed guardrail to collapse."

—FRANK WOESTE, VIRGINA TECH UNIVERSITY

"Most decks and guardrails collapse because they were not properly designed and constructed. It is practically impossible to overload a deck designed and built to the 40 psf live load requirement, or for a properly designed and constructed guardrail to collapse."

My Deck Is Not High Above the Ground

A deck that is high above the ground presents more risk than a deck that is close to the ground. This does not mean that a deck that is close to the ground is risk-free. Injury can occur during a fall from a surprisingly low height. A fall from a couple feet can cause serious injury depending on how you land. Guards are required when a deck is more than 30 inches above the surrounding area. This should provide a clue about the safety of low-to-ground decks.

Is My Deck Safe?

The purpose of this chapter is to help you understand that your deck may not be as safe as you believe it is. While the odds of being injured by a deck failure are low for most decks, the odds increase for some decks. For example, the odds increase with the age of the deck and for decks built without a permit.

One purpose of the next chapter is to help you understand what are and what are not decks. Some structures look like decks, but are not decks. Some structures do not look like decks, but really are decks. The other purpose is to introduce you to some of the most common problems that increase the odds that your deck is not as safe as you believe it is.

These days, most municipal building departments provide online access to local codes, statutes, and even interpretations of the codes. This can help you problem-solve on site, and it is especially useful as inspectors tend to be out in the field most of the day and have very limited availability for taking questions. Most have brief office hours first thing in the morning.

Chapter 2: What Is a Deck?

What is a deck? This may seem like a silly question. Most would answer that a deck is a wood-framed structure at the back of a house. That is one type of deck. For purposes of this book, we will use the following definition of a deck:

- A deck is a wood-framed structure located outside of the house.

- Other materials may be used for components such as decking, rails, and posts, but the basic structure is made using wood.

- A deck may be attached to the house, but a deck is an independent structure except at the point of attachment to the house (if any).

- A deck is located at least a few inches above the surrounding ground or other surface outside of the house.

How many code violations can you spot? This deck has some nice features and offers some tidy outdoor living space, but upon close inspection you will see that a few errors were made in its construction. A) The concrete footings are not of adequate diameter. B) The guard rail posts have been notched at the point of attachment to the deck joists—this weakens them greatly and can lead to guard rail failure. C) Although they are set onto 2 × 4 sleepers, the 5/4 deckboards seen here are too close to the ground. 5/4 pressure-treated deckboards generally are not rated for ground contact.

Using this definition, many structures are really decks. A deck may be on the front of a house, in which case it is usually called a front porch. A deck may be a landing and a stairway to a door. The point is this: if it is built like a deck, then it may be a deck. If it is a deck, it should be evaluated using the guidelines for decks regardless of how it is used or what it is called.

Evaluate structures such as this as you would evaluate a deck.

WHERE'S THE BEEF?

Some readers are too young to remember this hamburger restaurant catchphrase from the 1980s, implying that something is insubstantial or not worthy of consideration. Well, the beef in this book continues here. It is difficult to understand and use the information in this book without first understanding the information in Chapter 1 and Chapter 2. Please read these chapters. This book will make more sense if you do.

Decks Covered in This Book

The information in this book applies to most, but not all, decks. This book covers decks that are built on one level, and their attached stairs. This book covers decks where the length of the deck joists are less than or equal to the deck width. Refer to Figure 10 (page 48) in Chapter 5 for an illustration.

This book does not cover decks subjected to heavy loads, such as hot tubs, spas, and very large snowdrifts. Freestanding decks (those that are not attached to the house) are not covered in this book. In many cases, all that will be required for these free-standing decks is additional bracing. You should consult other references or consult a structural engineer if you have or are planning to build a freestanding deck, or if you have or are planning to build a deck that is not covered in this book.

What Is Not a Deck?

This is an important question because applying guidelines intended for one type of structure to another type of structure is not safe. A structure is not a deck if it is built using materials other than wood or other materials not approved for use as a deck component. If the structure is built using concrete, asphalt, stone, brick, pavers, or similar materials, it is not a deck. If the structure is supported entirely on the ground, it is not a deck.

Cantilevered Balconies: A Potential Safety Hazard

A structure is not a deck if the structural supports are extensions of the house floor joists. An extension of floor joists from the house is known as a cantilever, and this type of structure is a cantilevered balcony. A cantilevered balcony is supported by the house wall from which the balcony extends; the balcony has no other structural supports.

Cantilevered balconies can present more risks than decks. This is especially true if the balcony structural components are not visible because they are covered both above and below. Water can enter into concealed balcony structural components through or around missing or improperly installed flashing. Water will, over time, cause these structural components to deteriorate. Deteriorated structural components are more likely to fail, resulting in balcony collapse.

Cantilevered balconies are governed by different codes and standards. This book does not address cantilevered balconies. If you have a cantilevered balcony, especially if the structural components are concealed, *you would be wise to find a way to inspect these components*. Installing a removable panel under the balcony structural components where they project from the house is a good option. You would also be wise to install ventilation openings under the balcony to help the components dry if water leaks into the framing. Refer to other publications for information about installing inspection panels and ventilation for cantilevered balconies.

A cantilevered balcony.

Covered and Enclosed Decks

Decks are sometimes covered by a roof. They are sometimes surrounded by insect screens. Occasionally, someone will completely enclose a deck with solid walls. Deck construction guidelines, such as DCA 6 and the IRC, do not address the additional loads imposed by these components. These types of structures are not within the scope of this book. You should ask a qualified contractor, home inspector, or engineer to help you evaluate these structures.

Forces Acting on a Deck

A deck can move in any direction. It may not seem so, but you are not strong enough to move a properly constructed deck. Of course, if you push on a deck and it moves, do not use the deck. It is extremely dangerous.

Mother Nature, however, is more than strong enough to move a deck in any direction she wishes. Many people together can move a deck, but deck movement caused only by people standing on it is extremely unlikely.

Gravity is the most obvious force acting on a deck. Gravity exerts a downward force on the deck. When a deck fails, for whatever reason, gravity takes over and pulls the deck, and any occupants, down toward the ground. Gravity is not the only force acting on a deck, and it is not necessarily the most important force.

Decks move in a horizontal direction. A deck can move from side to side. A deck can move away from the house. The forces that move a deck in a horizontal

This is not a deck by our definition, but it shows a decklike structure that is settling and nearing collapse.

It take a lot of force to move a deck—this hurricane damage is an extreme example. The forces of nature that cause decks to fail tend to be subtler but are no less devastating.

direction are called *lateral loads*. Remember this term. You will see it again.

Lateral loads are caused in several ways. People can cause lateral loads, especially if they are moving in unison (do not line dance on a deck). Wind can cause lateral loads. Earthquakes and water movement can cause lateral loads. We cannot do much about lateral loads caused by earthquakes and water (floods). Lateral loads caused by people and wind are usually small and cause very little deck movement. These small movements can, over time, loosen the fasteners and connectors that hold the deck together and secure the deck to the house. Loose fasteners and connectors can fail, causing the deck to collapse.

Decks can move in an upward and downward direction too. Wind can lift a deck upward.

Footings that are located above the local frost depth can be subject to frost heave. Frost heave is caused when water freezes and expands. Frost heave can lift the deck upward. Some locations have unstable clay soil that can expand or contract with changes in soil moisture. Soil expansion and contraction can lift the deck upward, or cause the deck to move downward. Deck footings located on soil with an inadequate capacity to support the deck loads can move in a downward direction. Upward and downward movement of decks is often small, and these movements are usually not the primary cause of a deck collapse. These movements can loosen fasteners and connectors, and they can be a contributing factor of a deck collapse.

Rot and Corrosion

Wood rot (decay, deterioration) and metal corrosion (rust) are other forces acting on a deck. Deck components begin deteriorating from the first moment that they are exposed to moisture. Deterioration can begin during transport and storage. It certainly begins once the components are delivered to the job site. Rot describes the decomposition of wood by decay fungi. Corrosion describes the deterioration of metal by chemical reaction between the metal and substances in the environment. Rot and corrosion reduce the strength of components and will eventually cause them to fail. Wood and metal that present visible rot and corrosion are not safe and should be replaced.

All wood will eventually rot if exposed to enough moisture. Most wood is vulnerable to attack by wood-destroying insects, such as termites. Rot and insects are how nature recycles wood, so wood rot and

Severely deteriorated decking.

Cutting a chemically treated structural member breaks the protective envelope and leaves the cut ends of the board vulnerable. Apply preservative to all cut ends to increase the lifespan of your deck.

A little-known fact is that when the preservative chemicals are forced into the wood, the chemicals are absorbed in only a very thin layer at the surface of the wood. This has two implications for decks. One implication is that, sometimes, the layer is so thin that rot can begin sooner than it should. There is no way to know by looking at a piece of preservative-treated wood how thick or thin the preservative layer is. The other implication is that when you cut preservative-treated wood, the cut end has no protection against rot and insects. Cut ends of preservative-treated wood should be field-treated with a preservative such as copper naphthenate. This almost never occurs, so cut ends are more vulnerable to rot and insects. Never place the cut end of preservative-treated wood on or in the ground or embed the end in concrete.

Another little-known fact is that there are many levels of preservative treatment. Levels range from wood intended for dry interior locations to wood intended for submersion in saltwater. Beginning in July 2016, most wood intended for use in deck construction should be rated for ground contact, designated UC4A or better. Before July 2016, only wood that was actually in contact with the ground, usually just the deck posts, was required to be rated for ground contact. Wood that is not rated for ground contact should not be on or near the soil. There is no way to determine whether wood is rated for ground contact once the label on the end of the wood is removed. For wood purchased before July 2016, the best advice is that unless it is a 4 × 4 or larger, the wood should not be placed on or near the ground.

termites are good, so long as they do their thing somewhere other than at your deck.

Some wood species are naturally rot-resistant and insect-resistant. Note that rot-resistant and insect-resistant do not mean that these species will never rot, or that they are immune to insects. The heartwood of redwood and western cedars are the most common examples of naturally rot-resistant and insect-resistant wood used to build decks. Other wood species can be made rot-resistant and insect-resistant by forcing chemicals into the wood under pressure. Wood that is treated in this manner is usually called pressure-treated wood or preservative-treated wood. Most wood species can be preservative treated. Southern pine is one of the most common species of preservative-treated wood used to build decks.

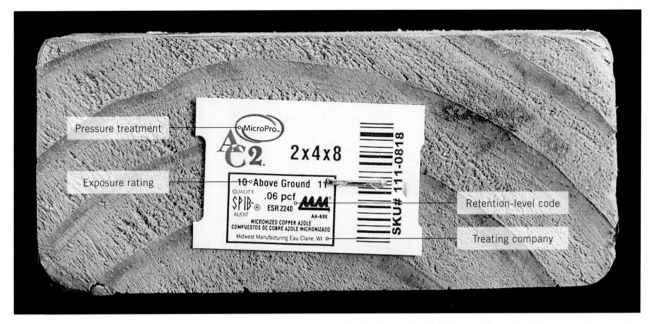

Pressure treatment

Exposure rating

Retention-level code

Treating company

Pressure-treated lumber labels list the type of preservative and the chemical retention level, as well as the exposure rating and the name and location of the treating company.

This joist hanger shows white rust and red rust. It should be replaced.

The most common chemical used to treat wood changed as of January 1, 2004. The chemicals used after that date tend to be less effective and, perhaps more important, tend to react with and corrode metal used for flashing, fasteners, joist hangers, and connectors in contact with preservative-treated wood. The implications of this chemical change are these: aluminum should not be in contact with preservative-treated wood produced after January 1, 2004, all metal in contact with preservative-treated wood should be either hot-dipped galvanized steel or Type 306 or Type 316 stainless steel, and metal in contact with decks built between 2003 and 2006 should be inspected regularly to detect corrosion.

Steel is the most common metal used for deck fasteners, hangers, and connectors. All steel, including galvanized steel, will eventually corrode if exposed to enough moisture, or if it comes into contact with another metal with which it is not compatible. Copper is an example of a metal that is incompatible with steel. Copper and steel should never be in contact with each other; the steel will corrode.

Galvanized steel is just steel that is coated with a layer of zinc. The zinc does not stop corrosion. The zinc sacrifices itself to keep the steel from corroding. Once the zinc layer is gone, the steel starts to corrode. The first indication that galvanized steel is nearing the end of its service life is when the component presents a white coating, sometimes called white rust. White rust indicates that the zinc is deteriorating. After the zinc layer is gone, the steel begins to rust. Rusting steel presents the common red rust color. When red rust appears on metal, the metal is weakened and should be replaced.

Did You Find the Beef?

After reading the first two chapters, you now have most of the tools that you need to start evaluating your deck. The final tool that you need is the ability to identify the parts of a deck and a stairway. Chapter 3 is a glossary of terms used to describe decks.

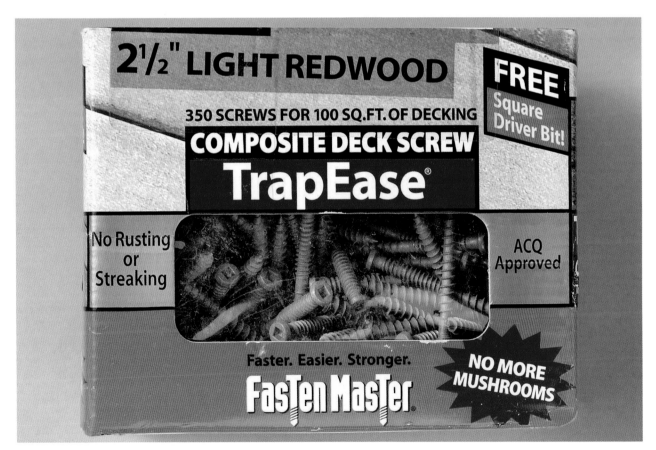

Make sure your fasteners will resist the corrosive effects of today's pressure-treating chemicals. Fastener manufacturers will usually provide this information on the product label.

Chapter 3:
Deck Anatomy

Just as a medical student must learn human anatomy, a deck student must learn deck anatomy. Fortunately, deck anatomy is much less complex than human anatomy. Each major deck component will be discussed in detail later in this book. The following deck anatomy lesson is an overview to get you started. This lesson assumes a wood-framed deck and a wood-framed house.

As with any building project, creating a safe and sturdy wood deck begins with understanding which parts are which and how they function together.

FIGURE 2:
Deck
Components

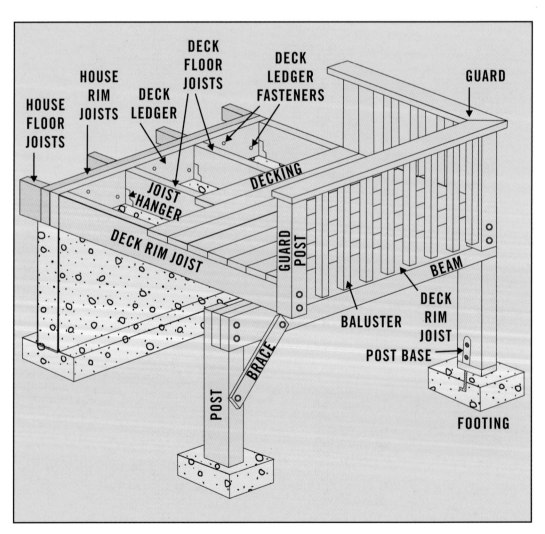

Parts of a Deck

Baluster (picket, guard fill-in): A baluster is a vertical component in a guard and in a stair guard that fills in the space between the guard posts. Deck balusters are usually made from wood 2 × 2s. Other materials may be used to fill in spaces between guard posts such as metal, wires (cables), wood composite materials, plastic, and glass.

Beam (girder): A beam is a horizontal structural member that carries a load imposed by other structural members, usually deck joists. Deck beams are usually made from two or more pieces of wood fastened together using nails or other fasteners.

Brace (bracing): A brace is a diagonal structural member installed between the corner posts and the beam in order to help keep the deck from moving (racking). Bracing is required if the deck post is more than two feet above the ground.

Cantilever (overhang): A cantilever is a horizontal extension of a structural component beyond its horizontal support. A cantilevered component has no additional support. Deck floor joists may be cantilevered beyond a beam, and a beam may be cantilevered beyond a support post.

Connector: A connector is a manufactured component that connects two or more deck components to each other. Common connectors are post caps, base caps, and hurricane clips. Deck connectors should be at a minimum hot-dipped galvanized steel. Type 316 stainless steel is recommended near saltwater.

Decking (floor boards): Decking is the horizontal component upon which you walk. It is usually made from wood, such as 5/4 × 6 and 2 × 6. Decking may be made from wood, wood composite materials, plastic, and metal.

Dimension lumber: Dimension lumber is solid wood that is sawn to specific sizes such as 2 × 10. The actual (nominal) thickness of dimension lumber used for most deck components is 1½ inches.

Fasteners: A fastener is a manufactured component that connects two or more structural members to each other. Common fasteners include nails, lag screws, and machine bolts. Carriage bolts are not approved fasteners for decks. Deck fasteners should be at a minimum hot-dipped galvanized steel. Type 316 stainless steel is recommended near saltwater.

Flashing: Flashing is a thin, flexible piece of metal, plastic, flexible polymer fabric, or similar material that does not allow water to pass through it. Flashing should be placed between the deck and the house, and at doors that open onto the deck when the deck is attached to the house. Properly installed flashing prevents water from damaging the wood that supports the deck at the house. Sealants such as caulk are not flashing. Sealants are not a substitute for flashing.

Joist (floor joist, deck joist): A joist is a horizontal structural member that supports the decking and provides the deck with some structural stability. Joists are usually connected to the ledger at the house and are usually connected to a beam.

Joist hanger (hanger): A joist hanger is a manufactured component that supports deck joists and beams. Joist hangers should be installed according to manufacturer's instructions, including using fasteners recommended by the joist hanger manufacturer. Joist hangers should be at a minimum hot-dipped galvanized steel. Type 316 stainless steel is recommended near saltwater.

Kerf (saw kerf): A saw kerf is a slot in a piece of wood that occurs when the saw blade is driven past the intended end point of a notch in the wood. Saw kerfs occur when wood is notched to create stair stringers or to notch deck joists when the joists are supported by a wood ledger. A saw kerf is a weak point in the wood.

Ledger (deck ledger): (1) A ledger is a horizontal structural member (usually a 2 × 8 or 2 × 10) that is attached to the house; the deck joists are attached to the ledger. (2) A ledger is a horizontal structural member (usually a 2 × 2) that is attached to a deck ledger or a beam to provide support for joists. Use of a ledger to support joists is not approved in some jurisdictions, and is not recommended.

Rim joist (rim board, band joist, band board): (1) A rim joist is a piece of wood around the perimeter of the deck; rim joists on the sides of the deck act as the first joist. (2) A rim joist is piece of wood around the perimeter of the house to which the deck ledger is attached. A rim joist is usually dimension lumber (often a 2 × 10) in older houses; it may be engineered wood in newer houses.

Flight of stairs: A flight of stairs consists of risers and treads between two landings.

Footing (footer): A footing is a structural component that transfers the deck loads from the deck post to the soil. A footing is made from concrete. Manufactured concrete blocks sold as deck footings are not acceptable footings. The bottom of the footing should be below the local frost depth.

Guard (guardrail, stair guard): A guard is a vertical component located around the deck perimeter to keep people from falling off of the deck. Guards are also required on the open sides of most stairs; these guards are sometimes called stair guards. Guards are usually made from wood, but other materials, such as metal, wood composite materials, and plastic, may be used.

Guard post: A guard post is the part of a guard that provides the primary resistance to loads that try to move the guard. A wood guard post should be at least a full-size 4 × 4 that is secured to the deck using a tension tie. Other materials, such as metal, may be used as guard posts.

Handrail: A handrail is a graspable component that runs along a stairway to provide support for people using the stairway. There are rules about handrail size and shape and about their location along a stairway.

Landing: A landing is a solid surface located at the beginning and ending of a flight of stairs.

Post (column): A post is a vertical structural member that transfers the deck loads to a footing. A wood post should be at least a 4 × 4; a 6 × 6 is better. Steel posts may be used.

Post base: A post base is a manufactured component (a connector) that secures the post to the footing so that the post does not move. A post base is the recommended method for securing the post to the footing. Other methods are allowed.

Post cap: A post cap is a manufactured component (a connector) that secures the deck to the post. A post cap is one method of securing the deck to the post. Other methods are allowed.

Riser: A riser is the vertical part of a stairway.

Stringer: A stringer is a diagonal structural member that supports stair treads. Stairs must have at least two stringers. Most deck stairs have three stringers.

Tread (step, stair tread): A tread is the horizontal part of a stairway on which you step.

Freestanding deck (nonledger deck): A freestanding deck is a deck that is supported only by posts and is not supported by the house. A freestanding deck is a good alternative when attaching the deck to the house is difficult or not possible, such as when ledger attachment through brick veneer is necessary. A free-standing deck may be attached to the house to provide lateral load resistance.

Lateral load connector (hold-down tension device, tension tie): A lateral load connector is a manufactured structural component that connects the deck to the house to resist forces that pull the deck away from the house. It is also used to secure a guard post to the deck. Examples include the Simpson Strong-Tie DTT1 and DTT2.

A Deck Is a System

Medical students and deck students share another common learning experience. They both must learn that the object of study is a system consisting of many parts, each of which can affect the other. A footing that is too small, or that is placed on poor soil, can sink. This sinking footing can cause the post to lower, which can cause the beam to lower, which can pull the joists away from the deck ledger, causing the deck to collapse. While learning about the individual deck components and their defects, it is important to remember that deck defects can be related and that a defect in one component can be caused by a defect in another component.

In the remaining chapters, we discuss the primary parts of the system in more detail. This will help you evaluate your deck, and it will guide you toward having a professional help you when necessary.

FIGURE 3: Deck Stair, Guard, and Handrail Components

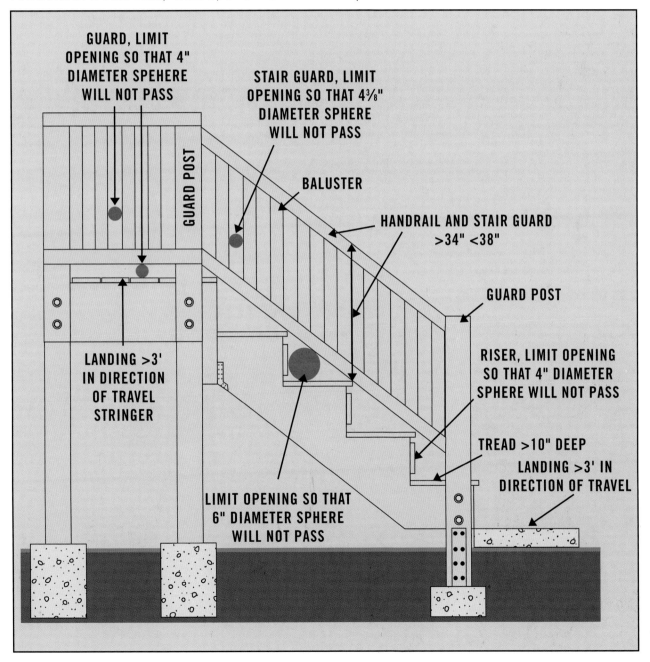

GUARD, LIMIT OPENING SO THAT 4" DIAMETER SPEHERE WILL NOT PASS

STAIR GUARD, LIMIT OPENING SO THAT 4⅜" DIAMETER SPHERE WILL NOT PASS

GUARD POST

BALUSTER

HANDRAIL AND STAIR GUARD >34" <38"

GUARD POST

LANDING >3' IN DIRECTION OF TRAVEL STRINGER

RISER, LIMIT OPENING SO THAT 4" DIAMETER SPHERE WILL NOT PASS

TREAD >10" DEEP

LANDING >3' IN DIRECTION OF TRAVEL

LIMIT OPENING SO THAT 6" DIAMETER SPHERE WILL NOT PASS

Chapter 4: Flashing

What Is Flashing?

Flashing is a permanent, low-maintenance barrier that stops water from entering into places where it will cause damage to wood and other house components. Flashing is different from sealants, such as caulk and roofing cement. Sealants may require replacement in as little as a year. Flashing, when properly installed, should last for many years. Sealants may be used in addition to flashing, but sealants should not be used as a substitute for properly installed flashing.

Flashing for decks built before 2004 is usually aluminum or galvanized steel. Both are acceptable materials, but both can corrode over time, fail, and require replacement.

Flashing for decks built since 2004 should be made from copper, one of the new flexible polymer materials, or PVC. Galvanized steel may be used, but this material can corrode over time. Aluminum should not be used because it can corrode rapidly when exposed to the preservative chemicals used to treat deck lumber.

Why Is Flashing Important?

Wood rot is a leading cause of deck failure. Wood rot is caused by decay fungi, which produce enzymes that dissolve and weaken wood. These decay fungi need water to survive. Once the moisture content of wood that is not preservative-treated, or wood that is not naturally decay-resistant, exceeds about 20 percent, decay fungi can grow and weaken the wood to the point of failure. Wood that is visibly rotted has already lost much of its strength.

Properly installed flashing protects wood by keeping water away from the wood. Wood that remains dry can last for a very long time.

House rim joist is rotted due to improper flashing.

Where Should Deck Flashing Be Located?

Deck flashing should be located at two places:

1. At any place where the deck touches the house

2. At doors that open onto the deck

Flashing for doors that open onto a deck should be integrated with the deck flashing.

Deck flashing is not required for freestanding decks that do not touch the house.

Where Should I Look for Water Damage Around Decks?

The most common location for water damage around decks is around doors that open on to the deck. The next most common location is anywhere that the deck is attached to the house.

Water damage usually presents as dark stains and as soft wood that you can penetrate with a screwdriver. Dark stains on the outside deck boards are often caused by dirt and debris. Such stains are rarely a concern. Dark

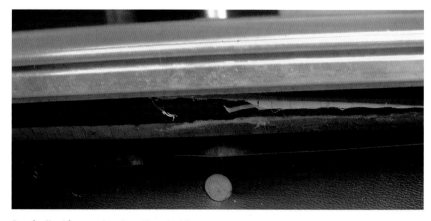

Gap in flashing under door threshold.

stains inside the house indicate that water has found its way in. These stains are a concern.

Look where the deck is attached to the house. Look inside the house where the deck is attached and any other place where the deck touches the house. Pay special attention to places where bolts or screws penetrate the interior wood. You may need to move insulation or ceiling tiles to look at these inside areas.

If the inside area has a permanent finished ceiling, such as drywall, look for irregular-shaped brown stains on the drywall.

Look on the exterior side of doors that open onto the deck, especially under the door and at the corners where the vertical jambs and the horizontal sill meet. Look inside on the floor around the door, especially at the corners.

SPOTTED IN THE FIELD

Water stains under an improperly flashed door.

Water damage under improperly flashed deck ledger.

Water stains on a ceiling.

How Should Deck Flashing Be Installed?

Flashing should be integrated with the water-resistive barrier on the house exterior wall and with other materials so that the material above is lapped over the material below. Lapping material higher on the wall over lower material creates a drainage plane, like shingles on a roof. Water that hits this drainage plane should drain harmlessly away from the house.

Figure 4 shows a side view of the current best practice for installing deck flashing.

Note the two types of flashing:

1. Water-resistive membrane flashing between the deck ledger on the right and the house sheathing on the left

2. L flashing on top of the deck ledger

Note that the water-resistive membrane flashing is under the water-resistive barrier above the deck ledger, and that the water-resistive membrane flashing is lapped over the water-resistive barrier below the deck ledger.

The illustration shows two washers located between the deck ledger and the sheathing. These washers provide a space for water to drain if it gets past the L flashing. Some experts approve this installation; others do not. This detail is optional and should only be used with sheathing, such as plywood and oriented strand board. This detail should not be used with insulating foam sheathing, or with sheathing that is easily compressed such as fiberboard sheathing. Check with your local building official to determine if washers are accepted in your area. Also note that installing washers changes the deck ledger attachment fastener spacing. This is discussed in the next chapter.

Figure 5 shows the current best practice for installing flashing at the deck door. Pan flashing is essential for diverting water that might enter under the doorsill or at the sill edges. Note that pan flashing installation takes place before the door is installed.

FIGURE 4: Current Best Practice for Installing Deck Flashing

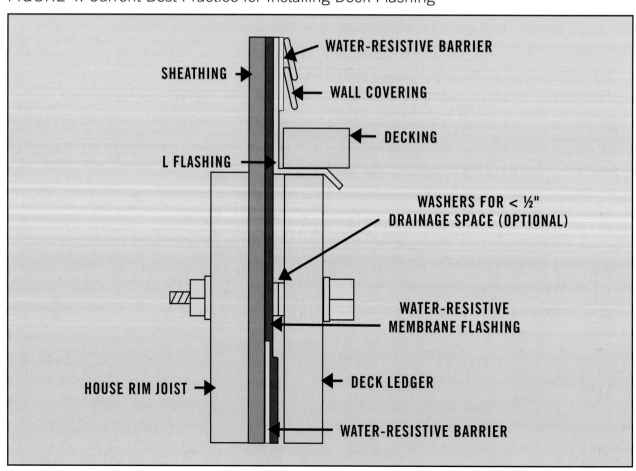

What Are Some Common Deck Flashing Defects?

Common deck flashing defects include:

1. No flashing is installed between the deck and house.

2. No pan flashing is installed at and under deck door threshold.

3. No flashing or sealant is installed where deck components (such as guards) penetrate wall coverings.

4. Flashing has gaps or seams that allow water to get behind or around it.

5. Flashing is not integrated with the water-resistive barrier, or with other flashing, to create a drainage plane.

6. Flashing is damaged and deteriorated.

7. Flashing relies on caulk, other sealants, or fasteners (such as nails) in order to secure the flashing to the wall.

8. Flashing is installed in front of wall coverings instead of behind the wall.

FIGURE 5: Flashing at Deck Doors

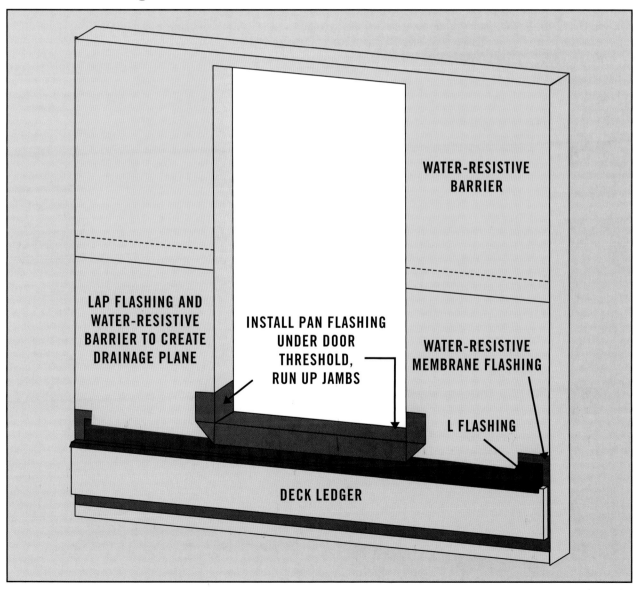

What Should I Do if There Are Problems with My Flashing?

Few decks or deck doors, especially older ones, will have flashing installed according to current best practices as described in this chapter. Whether this is a problem for you depends on which of several situations you find when you inspect your deck flashing and deck door flashing.

If deck flashing is installed, it will probably have either water-resistive membrane flashing or L flashing. Either type can work alone, but installing both types together provide better protection against water intrusion.

If the existing deck flashing is made from appropriate material, in good condition, properly installed according to current best practices, and there is no visible water staining or wood damage, then there may be no need to change anything.

If there is no deck flashing, you should install some even if you do not find water staining or damage. Sometimes, minor water intrusion takes time to produce visible stains and damage.

If a deck door has any flashing, it probably does not have properly installed pan flashing. If you see no flashing under the door threshold, the door has no pan flashing. Note that retrofitting pan flashing and ledger flashing at an existing deck can be a difficult and involved process. Doing this properly involves removing the door.

If your deck door has no pan flashing under the door threshold, applying sealant under the threshold can be an acceptable temporary solution in some cases. Read and follow the sealant manufacturer's instructions when selecting and installing a sealant under the door threshold.

Applying sealant as a substitute for pan flashing assumes that at least 1½ inches are between the bottom of the door threshold and the deck. This distance is necessary to help prevent wind-blown rain and water from infiltrating under the door. More distance may be necessary in climates where snow can drift against the door. The distance between the door

A cutaway view of ledger flashing.

Older houses were usually built using building felt (building paper) as the water-resistive barrier behind wall-covering materials. Newer houses are usually built with house wrap as the water-resistive barrier. Use the same material to replace a water-resistive barrier damaged during a ledger installation. L flashing provides another layer of protection that helps keep water from getting behind the deck ledger. Self-sealing membrane flashing is one type of water-resistive membrane flashing. A well-flashed deck will use all of these components.

threshold and the deck should be at least the likely snow depth, but not more than 7¾ inches (distance will vary according to local requirements) below the top of the door threshold.

If you find water staining or wood damage inside the house or at the deck ledger, then you will need to find the water source and stop the water intrusion. This may not be easy. Water staining and damage can appear far from the water source.

The steps you will need to take to repair faulty deck flashing or deck door flashing, or to install deck flashing and deck door flashing where none exists, will be different for each situation and are beyond the scope of this book.

If you are not sure about the best way to solve your deck flashing problems, you should consult with a qualified contractor or home inspector to determine your best course of action.

To apply self-sealing membrane, cut a piece to size and position it over the application area. Starting at one end, begin removing the thin plastic backing that protects the adhesive. Firmly press the membrane in place as you remove the backing, working along the installation area. To install long pieces of membrane, enlist the aid of a helper.

Install self-sealing membrane behind the ledger as protection from moisture. Lap the house wrap or building felt over the membrane from above as shown in Figure 4.

Chapter 5: Attaching a Deck Ledger to the House

What Is a Deck Ledger

Most decks use the house as one of the structural supports. To provide this support, a board called a *deck ledger* is usually attached to a part of the house floor system, specifically a rim joist. Refer to Figure 6 (see page 41) for an illustration. Deck ledgers are sometimes attached to the house foundation. Refer to Figure 9 (see page 46) for an illustration.

Why Is the Deck Ledger Attachment to the House Important?

When the deck ledger is attached to the house, this connection is an essential element of the structural integrity of a deck. Flashing helps maintain this structural integrity by preserving the strength of the wood and the fasteners. Without a solid connection between the deck and the house, the deck could collapse.

Install staggered fasteners on the ledger board using spacing specified in the table below.

LOCATION OF LAG SCREWS AND BOLTS IN BAND JOISTS AND DECK LEDGER BOARDS

	TOP EDGE	BOTTOM EDGE	ENDS	ROW SPACING
LEDGER	≥ 2"	≥ ¾"	≥ 2" & ≤ 5"	1⅝" & ≤ 5"
DIMENSION LUMBER BAND JOIST	≥ ¾"	≥ 2"	≥ 2" & ≤ 5"	≥ 1⅝" & ≤ 5"

Why Are Nails Not Allowed for Deck Ledger Attachment?

The 2000 edition of the IRC stated the following in Section R502.2.1-Decks: "Where supported by attachment to an exterior wall, decks shall be positively anchored to the primary structure and designed for both vertical and lateral loads as applicable. Such attachment shall not be accomplished by the use of toenails or nails subject to withdrawal." Subsequent IRC editions contain a similar requirement. Note that almost all nails used to secure a deck ledger to the house are subject to withdrawal. This is one reason why nails may not be used as the only method of securing a deck ledger to the house.

Recent research into deck collapses has determined that many collapses occur when the deck pulls away from the house in a horizontal direction, then falls vertically. Collapse in a completely vertical direction also occurs, but this is not as common. One reason why horizontal failures are more common is that nails have good resistance against breaking in the vertical direction, but they have very low resistance against pulling out from wood in the horizontal direction. A safe deck that is attached to the house needs a good connection in both the horizontal and vertical directions. Properly installed bolts or screws can provide part of the necessary connection; nails cannot.

Older decks were often attached to the house using only nails. This is a serious defect that should be corrected immediately. Decks attached to the house using only nails are much more likely to collapse as compared to decks attached using bolts or screws.

FIGURE 6: Structural Components of a House and a Deck

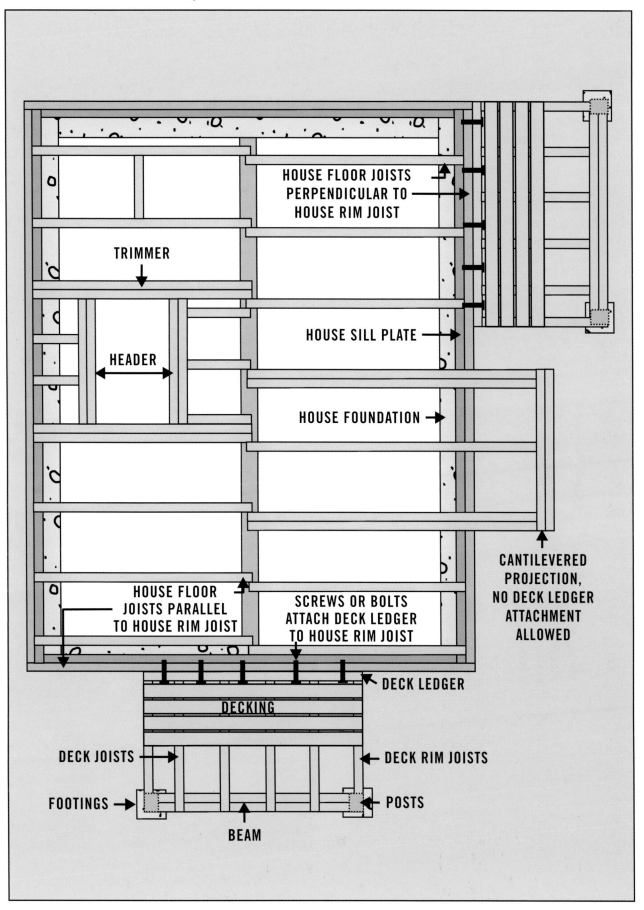

HOUSE FLOOR JOISTS PERPENDICULAR TO HOUSE RIM JOIST

TRIMMER

HEADER

HOUSE SILL PLATE

HOUSE FOUNDATION

CANTILEVERED PROJECTION, NO DECK LEDGER ATTACHMENT ALLOWED

HOUSE FLOOR JOISTS PARALLEL TO HOUSE RIM JOIST

SCREWS OR BOLTS ATTACH DECK LEDGER TO HOUSE RIM JOIST

DECK LEDGER

DECKING

DECK JOISTS

DECK RIM JOISTS

FOOTINGS

POSTS

BEAM

How Should a Deck Ledger Be Attached to the House?

Connecting a deck ledger to the house is complicated because there are many ways to build a house and many ways to connect a deck ledger to a house. For example, the floor systems in older houses, and in some newer houses, use dimension lumber floor joists (such as 2 × 10s). Newer houses may use wood I-joists or trusses as the floor system. The floor system of the house may be perpendicular to the house rim joist, or it may be parallel to the house rim joist. The deck ledger attachment guidelines assume that the house floor joists are perpendicular to the house rim joist.

Some people may want to connect the deck ledger directly to a concrete block foundation wall, or to a concrete foundation wall. All of these situations present different challenges for making a safe connection between the deck ledger and the house.

A safe connection between the deck ledger and the house requires correct installation of the bolts or screws. A deck ledger should be attached to the house rim joist using hot-dipped galvanized steel or stainless-steel machine bolts (not carriage bolts) or lag screws that are at least ½-inch diameter. All bolts

SPOTTED IN THE FIELD

Deck ledger secured using only nails. This is a very dangerous situation that should be corrected immediately.

SPOTTED IN THE FIELD

The deck ledger is secured to engineered rim board. House floor joists are I-joists perpendicular to the rim board. This is an acceptable connection if the bolts are properly installed.

Self-tapping ledger screws. These may not be approved in some jurisdictions. If approved, they must be installed per manufacturer instructions.

and screws should have washers at the appropriate locations. Bolts and screws should be installed into drilled holes that are not too small or too large. Holes for bolts should be about ⁹⁄₁₆-inch diameter and holes for screws should be about ⁵⁄₁₆-inch diameter. Screws should be installed by turning, usually with a wrench. Screws should never be installed using a hammer; this will severely damage the wood and create a loose attachment that could easily fail. The tips of all screws should extend beyond the house rim joist.

Note that other fasteners, such as LedgerLOK brand, may be used to connect a deck ledger to the house. These fasteners should be installed in strict compliance with manufacturer's instructions, as should all fasteners and connectors.

There are specific rules about the quantity and location of bolts or screws used to attach a deck ledger to the house rim joist. Table 1 (see page 44) assumes the following conditions:

1. Deck ledger is #2 grade or better, preservative-treated, Southern pine, Douglas fir-larch, or hem-fir, 2 × 8 or larger.

2. House rim joist is 1½-inch-thick spruce-pine-fir, Southern pine, Douglas fir-larch, or hem-fir (RJ), or 1- or 1⅛-inch-thick engineered wood (EW).

3. House floor joists or trusses are perpendicular to the house rim joist. Note that Table 1 (see page 44) assumes ½-inch-diameter bolts or screws. Table 1 (see page 44) and Figures 7 and 8 do not apply if larger-diameter bolts or screws are used.

TO COUNTERBORE OR NOT TO COUNTERBORE?

Should you counterbore the guide holes for lag screws when attaching a ledger? Good question. Traditionally, many deck builders and DIYers have employed counterbores so the lag screw head is recessed and out of the way of any joist hangers. Some think the appearance is neater too. But today, just about any inspector will tell you not to use counterbores. They base this on the fact that when structural members are tested to determine attachment protocols, they test the full thickness of the lumber. If counterbores are used, the thickness of the board at the point of attachment is reduced and you are actually weakening the holding power. A 2 × 8 with a ½" deep counterbore, for example, will have only 1" of wood at the point of attachment. The counterbore also provides unnecessary exposure and creates a spot for moisture to pool.

Another option for attaching ledgers is to use self-tapping ledger screws, which are now allowed by some jurisdictions. Typically smaller in diameter and featuring star-drive screw heads, these fasteners can be driven directly into the ledger and rim joist with no pilot holes. They are made from high-strength metal that outperforms the steel used in inexpensive forged lag screws. The low-profile screw heads do not interfere significantly with hanger installation. If you wish to use these screws, check with your building inspector first and confirm which size screw they recommend.

Do not counterbore lag screws or bolt heads and washers when attaching your deck ledger to your house. The counterbore holes remove wood, which has the effect of making the ledger thinner at its key connection points. On the plus side, countersunk heads allow you more flexibility in locating your joist hangers.

NOTE: Guide holes are being drilled too close to ledger end and edges.

The deck ledger should not be attached through any exterior wall covering, including siding, stucco, and brick. The deck ledger should be not more than one inch from the rim joist. This one inch includes wall sheathing, flashing, and any washers installed for drainage.

The house rim joist must bear directly on the house foundation, or on something, such as a framed wall, that bears directly on the foundation. Connection to a cantilevered projection beyond the foundation, such as a bay window or a wood-framed chimney, is not allowed.

TABLE 1: DECK LEDGER FASTENER SPACING

DECK JOIST SPAN	RIM JOIST TYPE	≤ 6'	6'1" 8'0"	8'1" 10'0"	10'1" 12'0"	12'1" 14'0"	14'1" 16'0"	16'1" 18'0"
CONNECTION SPECIFICATIONS				MAXIMUM ON-CENTER FASTENER SPACING (INCHES)				
½"-diameter lag screw,	1" EW	24"	18"	14"	12"	10"	9"	8"
≤ $^{15}/_{32}$" sheathing, screw tip should extend	1⅛" EW	28"	21"	16"	14"	12"	10"	9"
past house rim joist	1½" RJ	30"	23"	18"	15"	13"	11"	10"
½"-diameter machine bolt,	1" EW	24"	18"	14"	12"	10"	9"	8"
≤ $^{15}/_{32}$" sheathing	1⅛" EW	28"	21"	16"	14"	12"	10"	9"
	1½" RJ	36"	36"	34"	29"	24"	21"	19"
½"-diameter machine bolt,								
≤ $^{15}/_{32}$" sheathing,	1½" RJ	36"	36"	29"	24"	21"	18"	16"
≤ ½" stacked washers								

FIGURE 7: Summary of Requirements for Fastening a Deck Ledger to a House Rim Joist

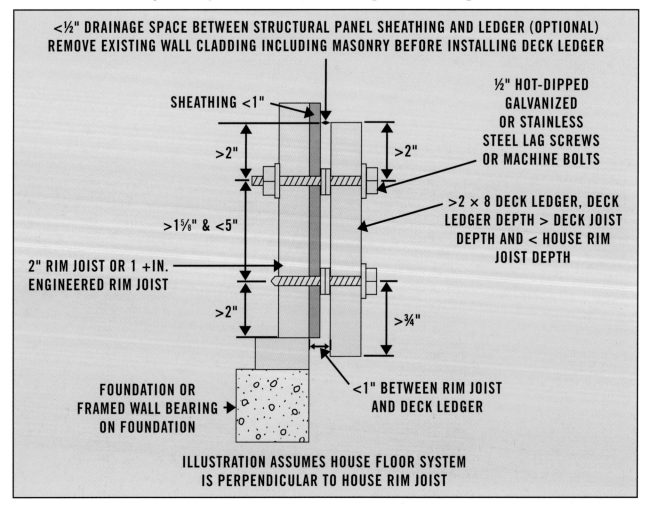

FIGURE 8: Deck Ledger Fastener Spacing Requirement (Refer to TABLE 1 for fastener spacing.)

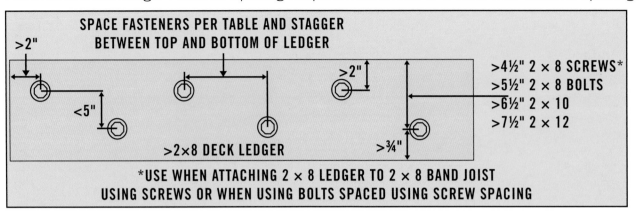

SPACE FASTENERS PER TABLE AND STAGGER
BETWEEN TOP AND BOTTOM OF LEDGER

>2"

>2"

>4½" 2 × 8 SCREWS*
>5½" 2 × 8 BOLTS
>6½" 2 × 10
>7½" 2 × 12

<5"

>2×8 DECK LEDGER

>¾"

*USE WHEN ATTACHING 2 × 8 LEDGER TO 2 × 8 BAND JOIST
USING SCREWS OR WHEN USING BOLTS SPACED USING SCREW SPACING

SPOTTED IN THE FIELD

Deck ledger may not be attached to cantilevered framing.

A deck ledger may be attached to some types of house foundations, specifically cast-in-place concrete foundations and solid-grouted concrete block foundations. Solid-grouted means the concrete block cores have been filled with a concrete mixture designed for filling concrete block cores. Deck ledger attachment to other foundation types, such as hollow concrete block, masonry, and stone, is not allowed unless an engineer designs the attachment connection.

Attaching a deck ledger to a foundation can be a good alternative in places where the deck needs to be below the deck door because of snow or wind-blown water. This attachment can be risky because following the fastener manufacturer's instructions exactly is essential. Following manufacturer's instructions exactly includes drilling and cleaning holes for the fasteners exactly as recommended. Failure to do so can allow the fasteners to loosen, withdraw from the foundation, and allow the deck to collapse.

A deck ledger may be attached to wood trusses under certain conditions. Refer to the installation details in Attachment of Residential Deck Ledger to Metal Plate Connected Wood Truss Floor System, which may be found at www.sbcindustry.com.

FIGURE 9: Deck Ledger Attachment to a Foundation

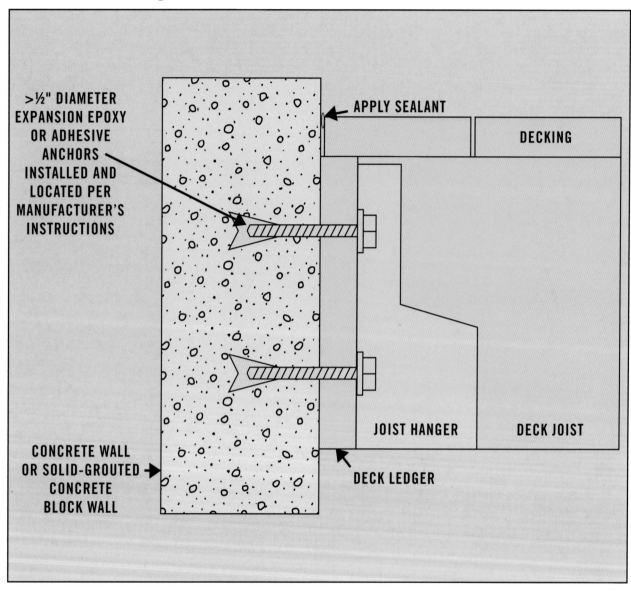

>½" DIAMETER EXPANSION EPOXY OR ADHESIVE ANCHORS INSTALLED AND LOCATED PER MANUFACTURER'S INSTRUCTIONS

APPLY SEALANT

DECKING

CONCRETE WALL OR SOLID-GROUTED CONCRETE BLOCK WALL

JOIST HANGER

DECK JOIST

DECK LEDGER

Are Lateral Load Connectors Required?

The 2015 IRC states in Section R502.2.1-Decks the following: "Where supported by attachment to an exterior wall, decks shall be positively anchored to the primary structure and designed for both vertical and lateral loads as applicable. Bolts and screws provide some resistance against lateral loads, but bolts and screws are mostly intended to provide resistance against vertical loads." The intent of this IRC section is that lateral load connectors should be installed on all decks that are attached to the house. Note that this requirement has been in the IRC for many years.

Deck ledger is secured to a floor truss. This floor system consists of trusses perpendicular to the deck ledger. This might be an acceptable connection if two bolts were installed in the truss.

How Should Lateral Load Connectors Be Installed?

Lateral load connectors should provide a total of at least 3,000 pounds of lateral load resistance. This requirement may be satisfied in one of two ways. One option is to install two 1,500-pound lateral load connectors. An example of this connector is the Simpson Strong-Tie DTT2. This option is most practical when the house floor joists are perpendicular to the deck ledger, when the connectors can be installed while the house is under construction and when the floor joists are dimension lumber. Even when practical, this option is difficult to install. This option can be installed under other conditions, but installation is much more difficult.

The other option is to install four 750-pound lateral load connectors. An example of this connector is the Simpson Strong-Tie DTT1. This option may be used regardless of the house floor joist orientation and of the house floor joist type.

All joist hangers, connectors, and fasteners should be installed in strict compliance with manufacturer's instructions. These instructions include using the correct fastener to install the joist hangers and connectors, and include using the correct joist hangers and fasteners for the application. Refer to manufacturer's instructions for details.

One instruction pertaining to installing the correct quantity of lateral load connectors is that the deck joist length is less than or equal to the deck width. This is sometimes known as the aspect ratio. Decks with other aspect ratios are not covered in this book and should be designed by a structural engineer.

FIGURE 10: Deck Joist Length Should Be Less Than or Equal to Deck Width

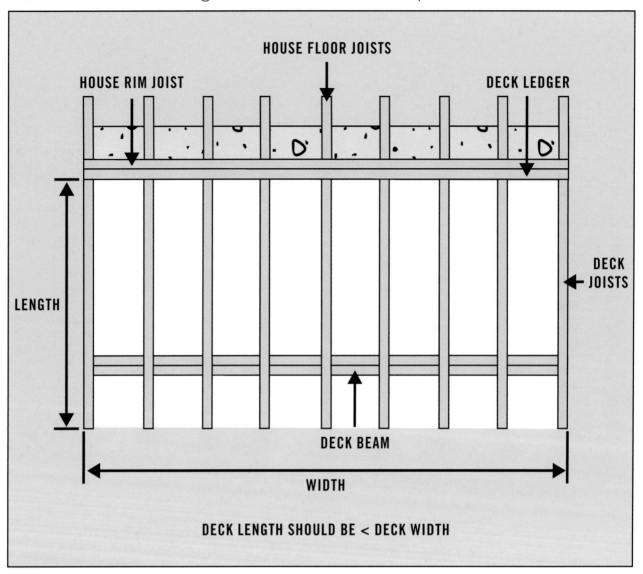

HOUSE FLOOR JOISTS

HOUSE RIM JOIST

DECK LEDGER

DECK JOISTS

LENGTH

DECK BEAM

WIDTH

DECK LENGTH SHOULD BE < DECK WIDTH

FIGURE 11: 1,500-pound Lateral Load Connector Installation

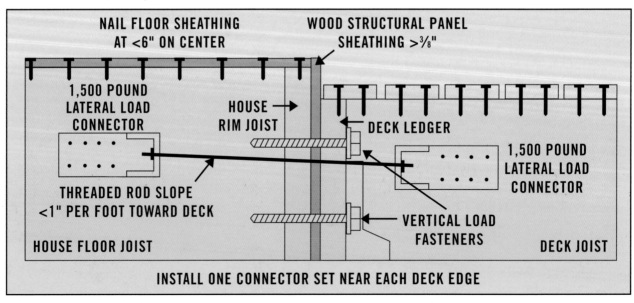

NAIL FLOOR SHEATHING AT <6" ON CENTER

WOOD STRUCTURAL PANEL SHEATHING >⅜"

1,500 POUND LATERAL LOAD CONNECTOR

HOUSE RIM JOIST

DECK LEDGER

1,500 POUND LATERAL LOAD CONNECTOR

THREADED ROD SLOPE <1" PER FOOT TOWARD DECK

VERTICAL LOAD FASTENERS

HOUSE FLOOR JOIST

DECK JOIST

INSTALL ONE CONNECTOR SET NEAR EACH DECK EDGE

FIGURE 12: 750-Pound Lateral Load Connector Installation

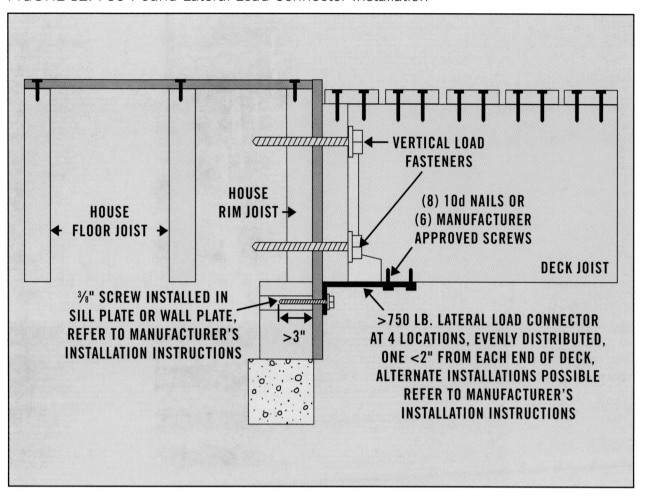

HOUSE FLOOR JOIST

HOUSE RIM JOIST →

VERTICAL LOAD FASTENERS

(8) 10d NAILS OR (6) MANUFACTURER APPROVED SCREWS

DECK JOIST

⅜" SCREW INSTALLED IN SILL PLATE OR WALL PLATE, REFER TO MANUFACTURER'S INSTALLATION INSTRUCTIONS

>3"

>750 LB. LATERAL LOAD CONNECTOR AT 4 LOCATIONS, EVENLY DISTRIBUTED, ONE <2" FROM EACH END OF DECK, ALTERNATE INSTALLATIONS POSSIBLE REFER TO MANUFACTURER'S INSTALLATION INSTRUCTIONS

Simpson Strong-Tie DTT1 installed.
Photo courtesy Simpson Strong-Tie.

What Are Some Common Deck Ledger Attachment Defects?

Common deck ledger attachment defects include:

1. Deck ledger is attached using only nails.

2. Deck ledger is attached through exterior wall coverings.

3. Deck ledger is attached to a cantilevered structure, such as a bay window.

4. The deck's fasteners, joist hangers, or connectors are improperly installed, corroded, or damaged.

5. Washers are not installed on bolts and screws.

6. Bolts or screws are too small.

7. Bolts or screws are spaced too far apart, or are not in the recommended location.

8. Bolts or screws are too close to the edge of the deck ledger, or rim joist.

9. Rim joist or deck ledger is not the proper material or size.

Deck ledger may not be attached through brick veneer. This is allowed in some jurisdictions. Lag screws are not staggered–another installation error.

Deck ledger may not be attached to an I-joist web. This is a dangerous defect.

Deck ledger may not be attached to an I-joist using a wood block. Carriage bolts may not be used to attach a deck ledger.

Half-inch diameter screws or bolts should be at least 2" from the edges of the deck ledger.

Deck ledger attachment bolts are not staggered as they should be.

●●●●●●

What Should I Do If There Are Problems with My Deck Ledger?

Deck ledger attachment is one of the most important safety issues for decks. Many deck collapses are the result of deck ledger attachment defects. The information in this chapter is intended to introduce you to this topic. If you believe that your deck and house fall within the guidelines in this chapter, installing bolts or screws and lateral load connectors as described in these pages will help improve the safety of your deck. If your deck and house do not fall within these guidelines, you should consult with a qualified structural engineer to determine your best course of action.

Chapter 6: Deck Stairs

What Are Deck Stairs?

Deck stairs allow access to the ground from the deck. Deck stairs are optional. Deck stairs may consist of one set of risers and treads, or the deck stairs may run to an intermediate landing before reaching the ground. Intermediate deck stair landings are small decks and should be built as such, including footings and bracing.

			EXAMPLE (39" High Deck)
1. Find the number of risers: Measure vertical drop from deck surface to ground. Divide by 7. Round up to nearest whole number.	Vertical drop: ÷ 7 = Number of risers: =		39" ÷ 5.57" = 6
2. Find riser height: Divide the vertical drop by the number of risers.	Vertical drop: = Number of risers: ÷ Riser height: =		39" ÷ 6 = 6.5"
3. Find tread run: Typical treads made from two 2 × 6s have a run of 11¼". If your design is different, find run by measuring depth of tread, including any space between boards.	Tread run:		11¼"
4. Find stairway span: Multiply the run by the number of treads. (Number of treads is always one less than number of risers.)	Run: Number of treads: Span: =		11¼" × 5 = 56¼"

Why Are Deck Stairs Important?

Deck stairs are important because accidents involving deck stairs, and all stairs for that matter, are common, and because these accidents are likely to cause serious injury. All deck stair requirements have been developed to help ensure that the deck stairs will be as safe as possible to use both when they are built and for years afterward. Complying with deck stair requirements is especially important for helping to ensure a safe deck.

How Should Deck Stairs Be Built?

Deck stairs should be built using 2 × 12 lumber that is made into stair components called stringers. Deck stairs may also be built using engineered wood that is intended for outdoor use and intended for use as deck stair stringers. You should check with the manufacturer before using engineered wood stringers.

Triangle-shaped pieces are usually cut from the wood to form the vertical parts of the steps called *risers* and the horizontal parts of the steps called *treads*. Cutting pieces from the wood creates cut stringers. Cut stringer tread boards are supported on the horizontal parts of the stringers. A less common method of making stringers is to use solid 2 × 12 lumber or engineered wood. These are called solid stringers. Solid stringer tread boards should be supported by 2 × 4s that are fastened to the stringers, or by manufactured tread brackets that are fastened to the stringers.

An important point to remember about deck stairs is that they are subject to the same requirements as interior stairs. Deck stairs and interior stairs should:

1. End at the top and bottom in a solid landing that is at least 36 inches deep in the direction of travel and is at least as wide as the stairs.

2. Not rise vertically more than 147 inches without a landing.

3. Be at least 36 inches wide.

4. Have treads that are at least 10 inches deep, measured between the leading edge of adjacent treads.

5. Have risers that are not more than 7¾ inches tall.

6. Not have a difference of more than ⅜ inch between any two riser heights and tread depths in a flight of stairs.

Note that tread depth and riser height requirements have changed over time and vary between jurisdictions. Deck stairs with different tread depths and riser heights are not necessarily defective if the tread depths and riser heights are consistent and vary by not more than ⅜ inch. A good rule is that if the stairs feel unsafe when you use them, they are probably unsafe, and probably should be repaired or replaced.

The maximum horizontal distance between stringer supports is six feet for cut stringers, and 13 feet 3 inches for solid stringers, assuming that the stringers are built using Southern pine 2 × 12s. Stringers that are too long may deflect more than they should when people use the stairs. Deflection can weaken stringer support connections, causing stair collapse.

The maximum distance between cut stringers is 18 inches, and 36 inches for solid stringers. If the deck stairs are wider than 36 inches, four or more stringers will be necessary.

Wood tread boards for cut stringers are usually 2 × 4, 2 × 6, or 5/4 × 6. Wider lumber dimensions, such as 2 × 8, may be used. Wood tread boards for solid stringers should be at least 2 × 8 for Southern pine, Douglas fir-larch, hem-fir, and spruce-pine-fir. Wider lumber dimensions may be used; however, wider dimension lumber used as tread boards and decking tends to cup more than narrower dimension lumber. Cupping is when the edges of the board curl up, creating a bowl in which water remains. Cupping can cause more rapid lumber rotting and can create a slip hazard when water remains in the cup.

FIGURE 13: Deck Stairs Requirements Summary

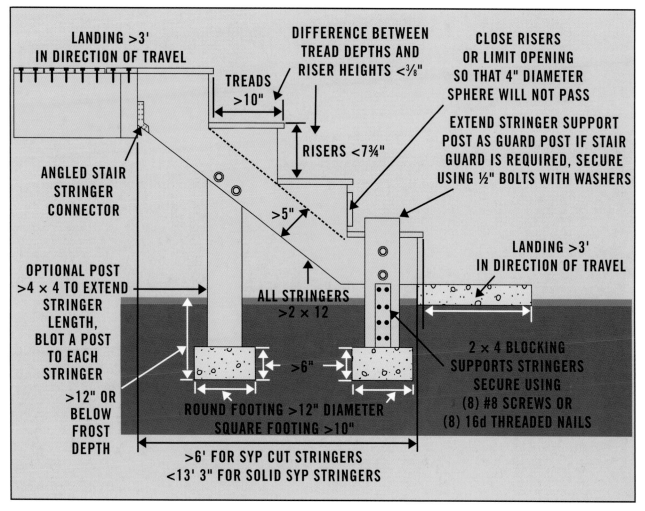

Tread boards may be made from manufactured materials other than wood, such as wood composite materials. All manufactured materials should be installed according to manufacturer's instructions. Manufacturer's instructions may limit the unsupported span distance, thus requiring that stringers be more closely spaced than 18 inches apart.

The space between the bottom edge of a cut stringer and closest point of the triangle cut is called the *throat*. A stringer throat should be at least five inches deep. Deck stair builders frequently over cut the triangle, leaving a saw cut beyond the triangle; this cut is called the *saw kerf*. The 5-inch depth measurement is to the saw kerf. A stringer with a smaller than recommended throat is weaker and may deflect more than it should when people use the stairs. Deflection can split the stringers causing stair collapse.

Stairs serving a deck that is high above the ground may have an intermediate landing between the deck and the ground. An intermediate landing should be built as a small deck complete with footings, posts, joists, beams, decking, and guards. The maximum vertical distance that a stairway may be built without a landing is 147 inches.

FIGURE 14: Deck Stairs Stringer and Tread Requirements Assuming Wood Tread Boards

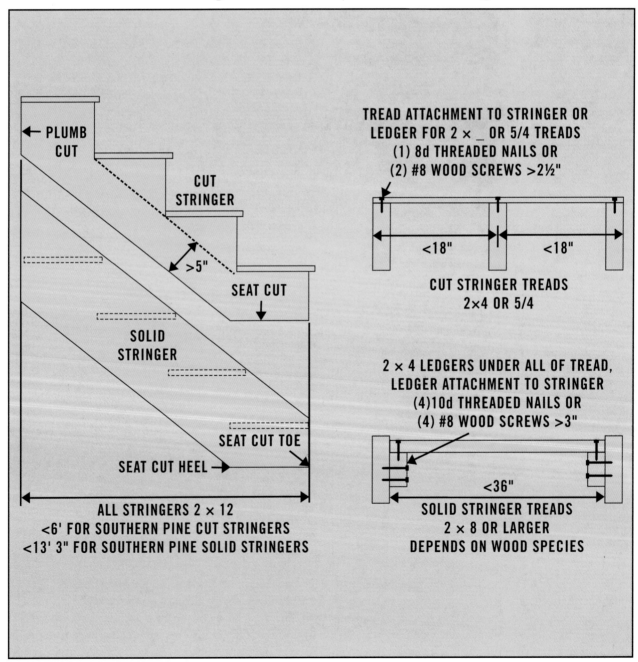

Stringer throat depth should be at least 5" measured to the saw kerf. This stringer is noncompliant.

How Should Deck Stairs Be Supported?

Deck stairs can deflect for many reasons. The first step in reducing deflection that can cause deck stair collapse is to ensure that the stringers are properly built as previously described, and to ensure that the maximum stringer horizontal span is not exceeded. Note that the stringer horizontal span may be reduced by installing posts and footings under each stringer as illustrated in Figure 13 (see page 55). Each post should be notched and bolted to the stringer as if it were a beam. Refer to Figure 26 (see page 84) in Chapter 8 for an illustration. The second step is to ensure that the stringers are properly supported at the top and bottom of each stringer.

If the stringers terminate at the ground, the stringers should be supported at the bottom of the stringers by a post and a footing as illustrated in Figure 13 (see page 55). This is, however, an uncommon installation detail. The next best alternative is to support the stringer seat (horizontal) cuts on a solid landing made from concrete. The bottom of the concrete landing should be below the local frost depth to avoid frost heave that can lift the stringers and loosen the stringer connection at the deck. This support by a concrete landing alternative may not be accepted in some jurisdictions, so discuss this installation with the local building official before proceeding. Stringers should not be placed directly on the ground, or on wood that is in contact with the ground; however, this installation detail is allowed in some jurisdictions.

FIGURE 15: Alternate Stringer Support Method on a Thickened Landing

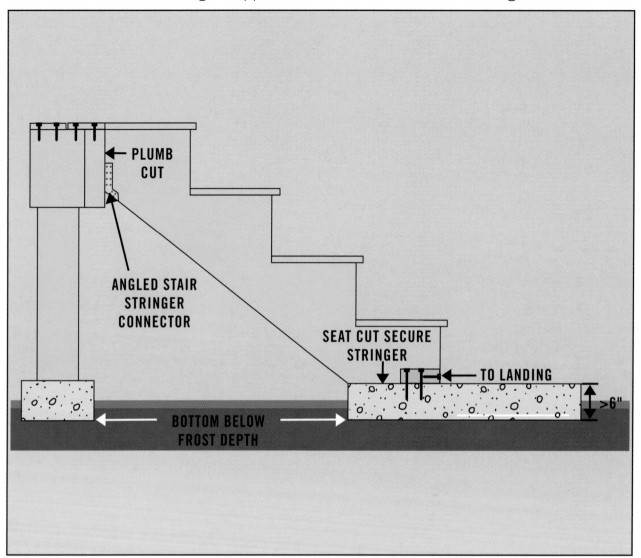

If the stringers terminate and are supported by a landing, the entire seat cut should bear on the landing. Some jurisdictions consider it acceptable if at least 1½ inches of the stringer seat-cut heel bears on the landing. A stringer should not bear only on the seat-cut toe. Bearing on the seat-cut toe could cause the wood to split along the grain and damage the stringer to the point of failure.

Stringers should be supported at the top of the stringers by an angled stair bracket that is installed according to manufacturer's instructions. An example of this bracket is the Simpson Strong-Tie LSC. Stringers should not be supported by straps, or by joist hangers or other connectors that are not approved by the manufacturer for supporting stringers.

Stringer support by angled stair brackets is an uncommon installation detail. Stringers are usually attached at the top of the stringer using nails. The

nails are usually inserted at an angle through the stringer into the deck rim joist, a technique called *toenailing*. The nails are sometimes installed through the deck rim joist into the stringer, a technique called *endnailing*. While these methods are allowed in many jurisdictions, neither method is recommended because nails have poor resistance against withdrawal in the horizontal direction. Nailed stringers that are pulling away from the deck are a common defect.

The entire plumb (horizontal) cut of the stringers should be in contact with the deck rim joist at the top of the stringer, unless the stringer is supported by an angled stair bracket that is installed according to manufacturer's instructions. Having the entire stringer plumb cut in contact with the deck rim joist provides a better bearing and attachment surface so that the stringer is more likely to remain attached to the deck rim joist. Stringers with less plumb cut bearing surface are more likely to shear along the woodgrain.

A stringer should not bear only on the seat-cut toe—the entire stringer end should rest flush on the bearing surface.

Toenailed stringer is pulling away from the deck.

Deck stair builders often like to use the deck rim joist as the last riser for the deck stairs. This makes installing the stair guards and handrail easier. This also makes it difficult to have the entire stringer plumb cut in contact with the deck rim joist. An angled stair bracket can solve this dilemma, but some deck builders use a drop header instead. One type of drop header is a piece of wood placed below the deck rim joist and attached to the rim joist using two pieces of lumber, usually 2 × 4s. Drop headers are not recommended, but if this type of drop header is used, it should be attached to the deck rim joist through the 2 × 4s using at least ⅜-inch-diameter machine bolts with washers. The drop header should not be attached to the deck rim joist using only nails.

Stringer plumb cut is not in full contact with deck rim joist.

Stringer plumb cut is not in full contact with deck rim joist and has sheared along the woodgrain.

Drop headers should not be attached using only nails.

Example of bolted drop header. Vertical 2 × 4 is split and should be replaced. Bolts should be located near the center of the 2 × 4 and should be located at least 2" from the bottom of the deck rim joist.

Is a Stairway Light Required?

A light is required for deck stairs. This light is often the same light that serves the door from the house to the deck. The light may be a floodlight if the floodlight is switched near the door from the deck to the house and if the floodlight illuminates the deck stairs.

Stair lighting. Deck stairs must be illuminated at night from a light located at the top of the landing. The light can be switch-controlled from inside the house, motion-controlled, or used in conjunction with a timer switch.

What Are Some Common Deck Stair Defects?

Common deck stair defects include the following:

1. Stringer plumb (vertical) cut does not fully bear on deck or other structural support.

2. Stringer seat (horizontal) cut is not properly supported.

3. Stringer seat (horizontal) cut is bearing on the seat cut toe.

4. Stringer is inadequately attached to deck using only nails.

5. Drop header is attached using only nails.

6. Stringer throat is too small.

7. Stringer horizontal span is too long.

8. Risers are too tall or riser height is uneven.

9. Treads are not deep enough or tread depth is uneven.

10. Stringer or tread boards are damaged, loose, or deteriorated.

11. Landing is not present at bottom of stairs.

SPOTTED IN THE FIELD

Cut stringer unsupported horizontal span is longer than 6'.

What Should I Do if There Are Problems with My Deck Stairs?

Adding support posts under stringers that are not 2 × 12s, are overcut, or are too long can be a good way to address these problems. Adding angled stair brackets at the stringer connections to the deck can sometimes be done without too much difficulty. Correcting riser height and tread depth problems usually requires replacing the stairs; however, these problems are uncommon causes of stair accidents. Uneven riser height and tread depth are a more serious problem and this usually requires replacing the stairs.

If you are not sure about the best way to solve your deck stair problems, you should consult with a qualified contractor or home inspector to determine your best course of action.

TIPS FOR USING METAL STAIR HARDWARE

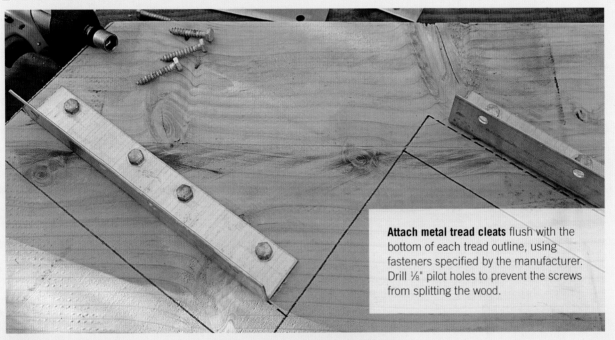

Attach metal tread cleats flush with the bottom of each tread outline, using fasteners specified by the manufacturer. Drill ⅛" pilot holes to prevent the screws from splitting the wood.

Hang the stringers from the rim joist of your deck with concealed stringer hanger hardware attached with 10d joist hanger nails.

Chapter 7: Guardrails and Handrails

What Are Guardrails and Handrails?

A guardrail is a component that helps keep people from falling from a higher elevation to a lower elevation. A handrail is a component that provides people with an object that they can grasp while using stairs. A handrail and a guardrail are usually combined into one component when installed on stairs. Guardrails on the open side of a stairway are sometimes called *stair guards*, in part because the requirements for stair guards are different from guardrails installed along a horizontal surface.

The technical term for a guardrail is a guard because a guard does not always consist of the rail-type vertical balusters people think of when they think about guardrails. A guard can be a full height wall or a partial height wall. Guard fill-in components can be the typical wood balusters, wire cables, metal balusters, wood composite materials, and even glass (safety glass, of course). A guard can be anything that satisfies the requirements for a guard. We will use the word *guard* in the remainder of this chapter.

Handrails, however, have specific requirements about size, shape, location, and installation. Handrails installed on deck stairs frequently do not comply with these requirements, even on newly built stairs.

Why Are Guards and Handrails Important?

Guards and handrails are important because they help prevent fall injuries. Fall injuries involving decks and deck stairs are among the most frequent, and among the most dangerous, of all the types of injuries that occur at home. People tend to lean against deck guards with the reasonable expectation that the guard will hold up against the pressure. Handrails are particularly important for children, the elderly, and people with impaired mobility. Watch someone from one of these groups use a stairway to get a feel for the importance of a properly installed and graspable handrail. Proper installation of guards and handrails applies to all raised surfaces and stairs, not just to decks and deck stairs.

Where Should a Guard Be Installed?

A guard should be installed where a walking surface is more than 30 inches above an adjacent surface within 36 inches. This includes the open sides of stairways that are more than 30 inches above an adjacent surface within 36 inches. Note that the 30-inch vertical measurement is to any surface within 36 inches, not straight down from the walking surface. This is because one may not fall straight down. Typical places where one may need to install a guard include decks, porches (including screen porches), and balconies. Note that insect screens are not guards.

FIGURE 16: Location Requirement for Installing a Guard

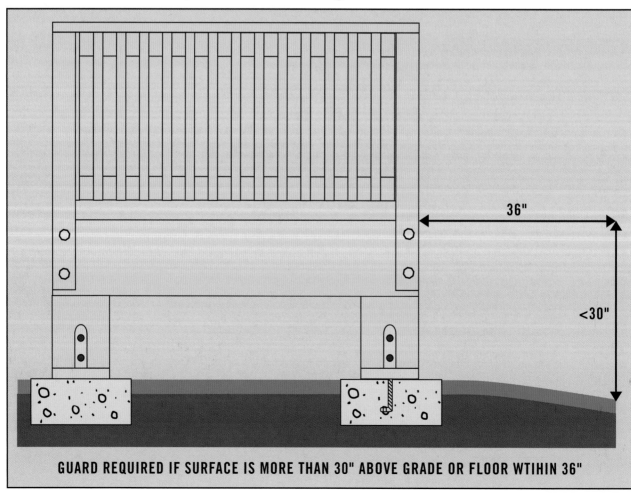

GUARD REQUIRED IF SURFACE IS MORE THAN 30" ABOVE GRADE OR FLOOR WTIHIN 36"

A screen porch should have a guard installed if it is more than 30" above a surface below.

A grippable handrail is secured to the guard on these deck stairs, meeting the grippable handrail code. In most areas you need the handrail on one side of the stairs only.

Where Should a Handrail Be Installed?

A handrail should be installed at a flight of stairs that has four or more risers. This includes the first and last riser in the flight of stairs. The handrail should be continuous from above the top tread to the leading edge of the bottom tread.

FIGURE 17: When a Stair Guard and Handrail Are Required

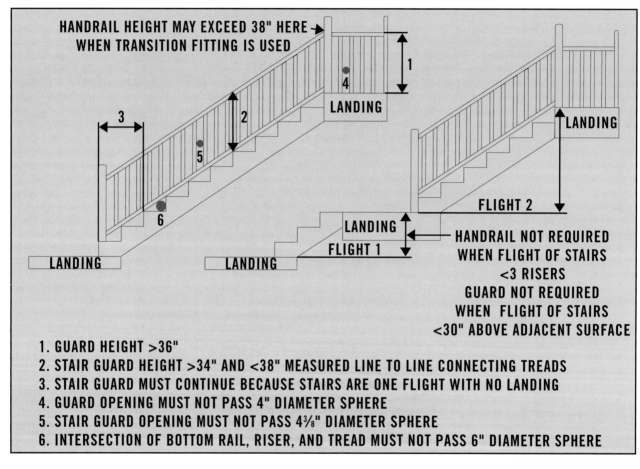

HANDRAIL HEIGHT MAY EXCEED 38" HERE →
WHEN TRANSITION FITTING IS USED

1
4
LANDING

2
3
5
6
LANDING

LANDING
FLIGHT 1
LANDING

FLIGHT 2
LANDING

HANDRAIL NOT REQUIRED
WHEN FLIGHT OF STAIRS
<3 RISERS
GUARD NOT REQUIRED
WHEN FLIGHT OF STAIRS
<30" ABOVE ADJACENT SURFACE

1. GUARD HEIGHT >36"
2. STAIR GUARD HEIGHT >34" AND <38" MEASURED LINE TO LINE CONNECTING TREADS
3. STAIR GUARD MUST CONTINUE BECAUSE STAIRS ARE ONE FLIGHT WITH NO LANDING
4. GUARD OPENING MUST NOT PASS 4" DIAMETER SPHERE
5. STAIR GUARD OPENING MUST NOT PASS 4⅜" DIAMETER SPHERE
6. INTERSECTION OF BOTTOM RAIL, RISER, AND TREAD MUST NOT PASS 6" DIAMETER SPHERE

How Should Deck Guards Be Built?

A deck guard at a horizontal surface should be at least 36 inches tall measured between the decking and the top of the guard. A few jurisdictions, such as California, require 42 inches.

Openings between deck guard fill-in components, such as balusters, should not allow a four-inch diameter sphere to pass. This includes any space below the balusters or other fill-in components, and it includes the space under benches and other built-in seating. It also includes any space between the guard and the house or other structure.

The performance requirement for a guard is that it not fail when 200 pounds of pressure is applied in any direction along the top of the guard. The performance requirement for guard fill-in components is that they not fail when 50 pounds of pressure is applied in a horizontal direction over a one square foot area. These performance requirements are meaningless without laboratory testing to determine how to comply. Fortunately, such testing has occurred and guidelines exist that can be used to build deck guards that comply with the performance requirements.

The following deck guard construction materials and techniques have been tested and demonstrated to comply with the performance requirements when properly installed, maintained, and when regularly inspected. Other materials and techniques may comply, but you should not rely on compliance unless the materials and techniques have been tested.

A deck guard post should be at least 4 × 4 preservative-treated Southern pine that is free from significant defects and has not been notched. Other wood with similar characteristics may be used. The posts should be located not more than six feet apart.

Several methods can be used for attaching guard posts to the deck. All of the methods require using at least one hold-down anchor attached to something other than the deck rim joist. An example of a hold-down anchor is the Simpson Strong-Tie DTT2Z.

Space under a guard should not allow a 4"-diameter sphere to pass.

FIGURE 18: Deck Guard Post and Baluster Construction

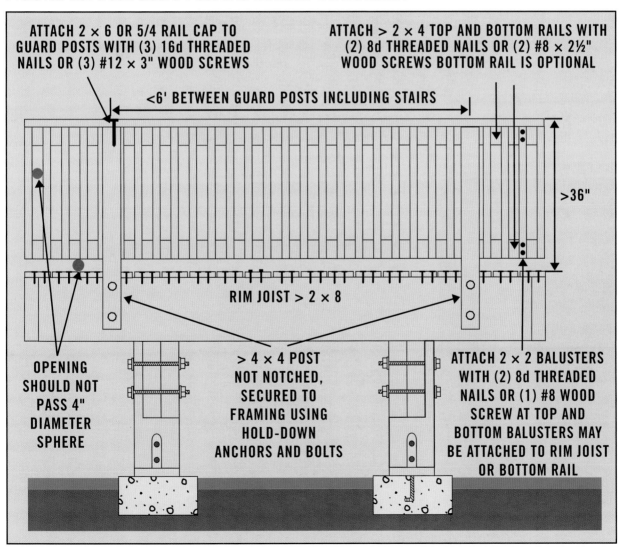

ATTACH 2 × 6 OR 5/4 RAIL CAP TO GUARD POSTS WITH (3) 16d THREADED NAILS OR (3) #12 × 3" WOOD SCREWS

ATTACH > 2 × 4 TOP AND BOTTOM RAILS WITH (2) 8d THREADED NAILS OR (2) #8 × 2½" WOOD SCREWS BOTTOM RAIL IS OPTIONAL

<6' BETWEEN GUARD POSTS INCLUDING STAIRS

>36"

RIM JOIST > 2 × 8

OPENING SHOULD NOT PASS 4" DIAMETER SPHERE

> 4 × 4 POST NOT NOTCHED, SECURED TO FRAMING USING HOLD-DOWN ANCHORS AND BOLTS

ATTACH 2 × 2 BALUSTERS WITH (2) 8d THREADED NAILS OR (1) #8 WOOD SCREW AT TOP AND BOTTOM BALUSTERS MAY BE ATTACHED TO RIM JOIST OR BOTTOM RAIL

There are other manufacturers. Note that these methods assume that the deck guard height is not more than 36 inches.

A guard post that is attached only to the rim joist is likely to fail by pulling the rim joist itself away from the deck. This occurs because the deck rim joist is often only secured to the deck joists and is often secured using only nails. Nails have very low resistance to withdrawal, especially when attached to the ends of joists. Even screws do not have enough resistance to withdrawal to comply with the 200-pound performance requirement.

Deck guard balusters are usually wood 2 × 2s. Attaching the balusters as shown in Figure 18

SPOTTED IN THE FIELD

This deck guard has more than 6' between guard posts making it noncompliant.

Notched deck guard posts can split at the notch and fail.

FIGURE 19: Deck Guard Post Attachment When Post Aligns with Deck Joist

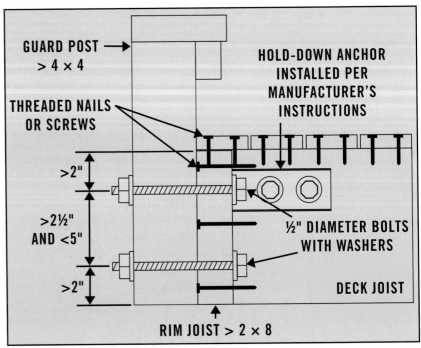

GUARD POST
> 4 × 4

HOLD-DOWN ANCHOR INSTALLED PER MANUFACTURER'S INSTRUCTIONS

THREADED NAILS OR SCREWS

>2"

>2½" AND <5"

>2"

½" DIAMETER BOLTS WITH WASHERS

DECK JOIST

RIM JOIST > 2 × 8

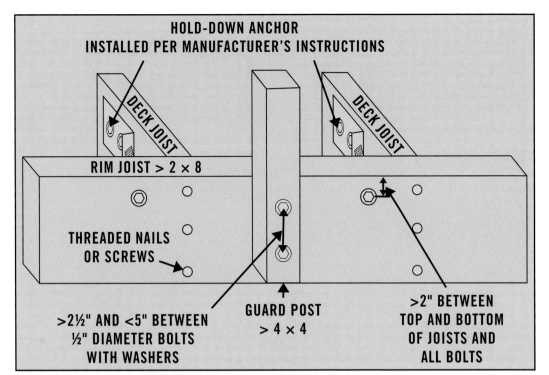

FIGURE 20: Deck Guard Post Attachment When Post Does Not Align with Deck Joist

HOLD-DOWN ANCHOR INSTALLED PER MANUFACTURER'S INSTRUCTIONS

DECK JOIST

RIM JOIST > 2 × 8

THREADED NAILS OR SCREWS

>2½" AND <5" BETWEEN ½" DIAMETER BOLTS WITH WASHERS

GUARD POST > 4 × 4

>2" BETWEEN TOP AND BOTTOM OF JOISTS AND ALL BOLTS

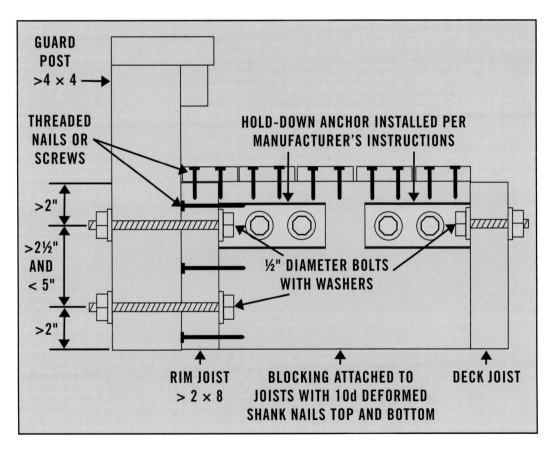

FIGURE 21: Deck Guard Post Attachment When Deck Joists Are Parallel to Rim Joist

GUARD POST >4 × 4

THREADED NAILS OR SCREWS

HOLD-DOWN ANCHOR INSTALLED PER MANUFACTURER'S INSTRUCTIONS

>2"

>2½" AND < 5"

>2"

½" DIAMETER BOLTS WITH WASHERS

RIM JOIST > 2 × 8

BLOCKING ATTACHED TO JOISTS WITH 10d DEFORMED SHANK NAILS TOP AND BOTTOM

DECK JOIST

should comply with the deck guard fill-in component requirements.

Materials other than wood may be used for deck guard fill-in components, and orientations other than vertical are allowed. Horizontal fill-in components, such as metal rods and cables, are allowed. Be aware, however, that children can climb horizontal fill-in components and that this could constitute a fall hazard. Materials such as thin wood lattice may not be used for guard fill-in components if the lattice does not comply with the fill-in components' 50-pound-per-square-foot performance requirement.

How Should Deck Stair Guards and Handrails Be Installed?

Deck guard posts should be located not more than 6' apart, including stair guards. The upper section of these stairs is more than 6' long without support.

Deck stair guards are subject to the same performance requirements as horizontal guards. Complying with the 200-pound load requirement is more difficult with deck stair guards because there are often no deck joists to which the deck stair guard posts may be attached. The deck stair guard post at the top of the stairs should be attached to the deck as described in Figures 19, 20, or 21 (see pages 70 and 71). The deck stair guard post at the bottom of the stairs should be attached to the stair footing as described in Figure 13 (see page 55) in Chapter 6.

Deck stair guard posts should be located not more than six feet apart, just as for deck guard posts. The only practical attachment method for intermediate deck stair guard posts is to attach the post to the stair stringer using at least two ½-inch diameter machine bolts with washers at each end.

Deck stair guard and handrail height should be between 34 inches and 38 inches measured from a line connecting the tread leading edges to the top of the handrail or guard. Openings between deck stair guard fill-in components should not allow

A deck stair guard should be at least 34" above the tread leading edge.

a 4⅜-inch diameter sphere to pass. If there is an opening between a deck stair guard bottom rail and the triangle formed by the riser, tread, and bottom rail, the opening should not allow a six-inch diameter sphere to pass. See Figure 17 (see page 68).

Deck stair handrails are subject to all of the requirements for interior stair handrails. These requirements include a graspable handrail shape, that the handrail be continuous from the beginning of the top riser to the end of the bottom tread, and that the handrail ends in a return or newel post. A return is when the handrail changes shape at the end of the handrail to provide a place for someone to grasp and to ensure that clothing, purse straps, and similar objects are less likely to get caught on the handrail and cause a fall. These requirements are all there to improve safety, and failure to comply with these requirements makes a deck less safe.

The typical deck stair handrail is a 2 × 4, a 5/4 × 4, or a 5/4 × 6 installed on top of the stair guard. None of these shapes are graspable, especially by children, and by adults with small hands or who have a weak grip, such as those with mobility issues. Almost all deck stair handrails are, therefore, improperly installed. Code officials usually pass this improper installation, even though the code requirements are clear about handrail requirements.

A 6"-diameter sphere should not pass through this triangle.

SPOTTED IN THE FIELD

The handrail in this picture is not one of the graspable shapes, is not continuous to above the last tread, and does not terminate in a return or a newel post.

FIGURE 22: Deck Handrail Shapes

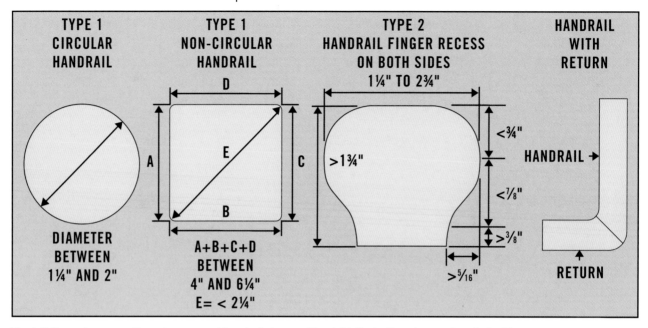

The left three shapes are the only approved handrail shapes. The right illustration shows a handrail with a return.

What Are Some Common Deck Guard and Handrail Defects?

Common deck guard and handrail defects include the following:

1. Handrail or guard is not installed.

2. Handrail grip surface is wrong size or shape (not graspable).

3. Handrail or guard is loose.

4. Handrail is deteriorated and has splinters.

5. Handrail is not continuous over entire flight of stairs.

6. Guard or handrail is not tall enough.

7. Guard post is notched at attachment to deck.

8. Guard post is nailed or screwed to deck.

9. Guard fill-in components are spaced too far apart.

10. Guard posts are too far apart.

What Should I Do if There are Problems with My Deck Guards and Handrails?

Deck guard and handrail defects are often some of the easiest defects to correct. Guard posts can usually be added or replaced using the guidelines in this chapter. There are several methods of attaching a graspable handrail to existing deck stairs. Attaching metal handrail brackets and installing any of the manufactured graspable handrails will work.

If you are not sure about the best way to solve your deck guard and handrail problems, you should consult with a qualified contractor or home inspector to determine your best course of action.

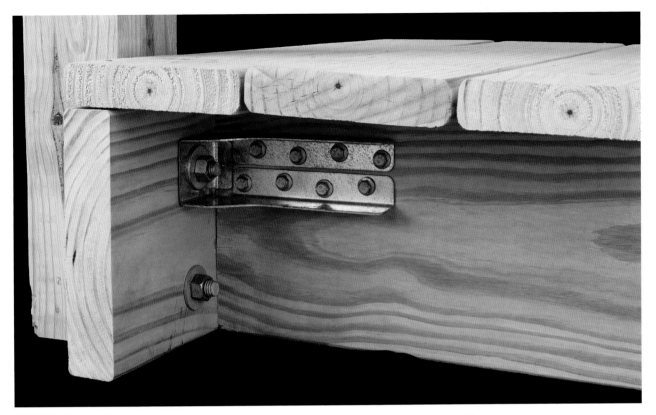

Deck guard support posts should be secured using attachment hardware for long-term strength.

 TIP: HOW TO LAY OUT STAIR STRINGERS

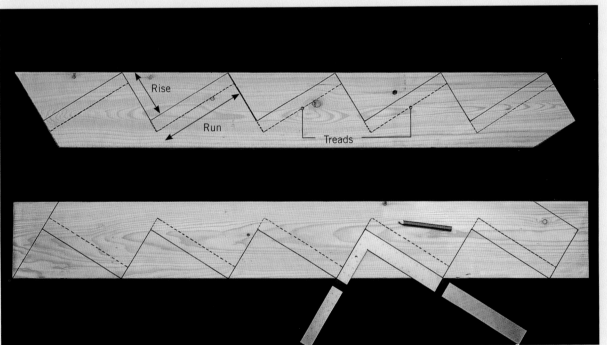

Lay out the stair stringers. Use tape to mark the rise measurement on one leg of a framing square, and the run measurement on the other leg. Beginning at one end of the stringer, position the square with tape marks flush to the edge of the board, and outline the rise and run for each step. Then draw in the tread outline against the bottom of each run line. Use a circular saw to trim the end of the stringers as shown. (When cutting the stringers for stairs without metal cleats, just cut on the solid lines.)

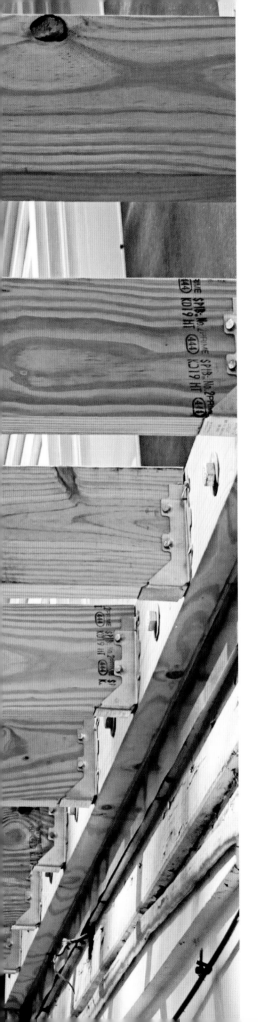

Chapter 8:
Deck Framing

What Is Deck Framing?

We define deck framing to include the deck joists, deck beams, decking, and the fasteners, connectors, and joist hangers that hold the deck together. Other deck structural components are discussed in other chapters. The deck ledger at the house is discussed in Chapter 5. Deck posts, bracing, and footings are discussed in Chapter 9.

Why Is Deck Framing Important?

As discussed in Chapter 3, a deck is a system. While it is uncommon to trace a deck failure directly to deck framing installation defects, these defects can, over time, contribute to deck failures by placing stress on the deck system.

Deteriorated deck framing components are another common cause of deck failure. Rusted fasteners, connectors, joist hangers, and deteriorated wood are weaker than intended. Fasteners can be particularly troubling because much of the deterioration is usually concealed and cannot be seen without removing the fasteners. Fasteners are sometimes so badly deteriorated that they provide none of the intended support and connecting capabilities. Rust is a particularly serious problem for decks near salt water.

How Should Deck Joists Be Installed?

Properly installing deck joists starts with selecting the species and grade of the lumber. Southern pine is used in many parts of the country and is by far the predominant species in the East. Various species of fir such as Douglas fir, hem-fir, and spruce-pine-fir are used, mostly in the West. Other wood species and engineered wood may be used. Most wood must be preservative treated for use outdoors. The exceptions are the heartwood of naturally durable wood species such as redwood. Number two grade or better is specified for all dimension lumber used when building decks. A grade stamp showing the species, grade, and other information should be found on every piece of dimension lumber.

The next step is to determine the joist span distance between supports, which is usually measured between the beam and the deck ledger. Once the joist length and lumber species are known, Table 2 may be used to determine the lumber size, deck joist on-center spacing, and the maximum allowable cantilever, if any. Note that while 2 × 6 deck joists are allowed, deck ledgers and deck rim joists should be at least 2 × 8.

SPOTTED IN THE FIELD

Fasteners are significantly rusted and should be replaced immediately. Fasteners showing any rust should be replaced.

Lumber grade stamp; this is No. 2 grade Southern pine, not preservative treated.

FIGURE 23: Measuring Deck Joist Span

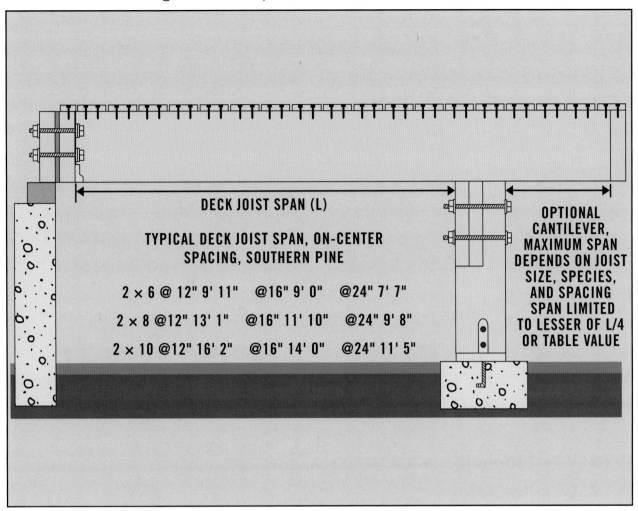

DECK JOIST SPAN (L)

TYPICAL DECK JOIST SPAN, ON-CENTER SPACING, SOUTHERN PINE

2 × 6 @ 12" 9' 11"   @16" 9' 0"   @24" 7' 7"

2 × 8 @12" 13' 1"   @16" 11' 10"   @24" 9' 8"

2 × 10 @12" 16' 2"   @16" 14' 0"   @24" 11' 5"

OPTIONAL CANTILEVER, MAXIMUM SPAN DEPENDS ON JOIST SIZE, SPECIES, AND SPACING SPAN LIMITED TO LESSER OF L/4 OR TABLE VALUE

TABLE 2: DECK JOIST MAXIMUM SPAN DISTANCE

WOOD SPECIES	LUMBER SIZE	DECK JOIST ON-CENTER SPACING					
		12"	16"	24"	12"	16"	24"
		MAXIMUM JOIST SPAN DISTANCE			MAXIMUM JOIST CANTILEVER		
Southern Pine	2 × 6	9'11"	9'0"	7'7"	1'0"	1'1"	1'3"
	2 × 8	13'1"	11'10"	9'8"	1'10"	2'0"	2'4"
	2 × 10	16'2"	14'0"	11'5"	3'1"	3'5"	2'10"
	2 × 12	18'0"	16'6"	13'6"	4'6"	4'2"	3'4"
Douglas Fir-Larch, Hem-Fir, Spruce-Pine-Fir	2 × 6	9'6"	8'4"	6'10"	0'1"	1'0"	1'2"
	2 × 8	12'6"	11'1"	9'1"	1'8"	1'10"	2'2"
	2 × 10	13'6"	13'7"	11'1"	2'10"	3'2"	2'9"
	2 × 12	18'0"	15'9"	12'10"	3'7"	3'9"	3'1"

Deck joists are often installed on the top of the deck beam. The other alternative is to install the deck joists flush with the top of the deck beam. Both methods are shown in Figure 24. Both methods are acceptable. Note that supporting a deck joist at the beam using a 2 × 2 ledger is not a recommended method. This method is common practice and is allowed in many jurisdictions; however, this method may not work as well under the wet conditions encountered outdoors as it works under dry conditions indoors.

FIGURE 24: Deck Joist Support at Deck Beam

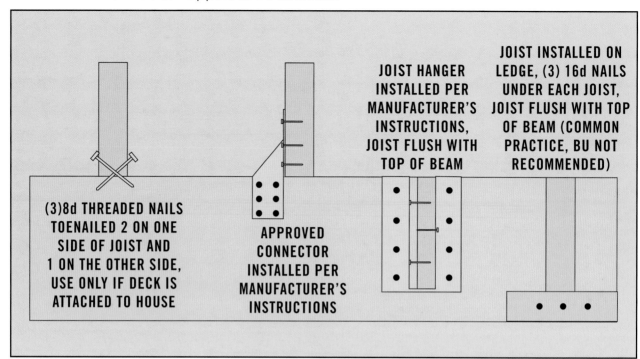

Deck joists should be supported at the deck ledger using joist hangers. Joist hangers are also the recommended support method when the deck joists are installed flush with the top of the deck beam. Supporting the deck joist at the deck ledger or deck beam by a 2 × 2 ledger or by an angle bracket are both common practice, but neither are recommended. Deck joists should not be supported using only nails.

Deck joists may be notched at the ends up to 25 percent of the actual joist depth. For example, a 2 × 8 joist (actual depth 7½ inches) may be notched up to 1⅞ inches. Measurement is to the saw kerf. Deck joists are frequently over-notched when supported at wood ledgers. Over-notched deck joists are weaker and will not bear the intended load.

Joist hangers should be installed according to manufacturer's instructions. Common failures to comply with manufacturer's instructions

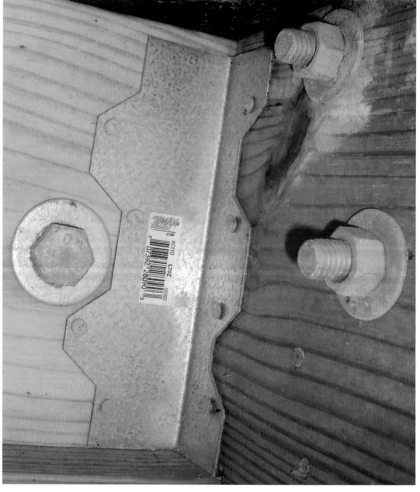

Deck joists and beams should not be supported by a plain angle bracket—use a rated joist hanger.

Deck joists should not be supported using only nails.

This 2 × 10 floor joist is significantly over-notched.

include not using the recommended fasteners and locating the joist more than ⅛ inch from the supporting deck beam or deck ledger. Screws should not be used to install any joist hanger or connector unless the manufacturer's instructions allow use of screws. Deck screws should not be used to install any joist hanger or connector. Table 3 shows minimum joist hanger requirements. Note that the joist hanger models in this table are current as of the publication date of this book. Confirm specifications and installation instructions with the joist hanger manufacturer. There are other joist hanger manufacturers.

 TABLE 3: JOIST HANGER REQUIREMENTS

DECK JOIST SIZE	MINIMUM HANGER CAPACITY (POUNDS)	TYPICAL SIMPSON STRONG-TIE MODELS
2 × 6	400	LUS26Z, LUC26Z
2 × 8	500	LUS26Z, LUC26Z, LUS28Z, LUC28Z
2 × 10	600	LUS28Z, LUC28Z, LUS210Z, LUC210Z
2 × 12	700	LUS210Z, LUC210Z

How Should a Deck Beam Be Installed?

Deck beams are usually built-up beams made from two or more pieces of dimension lumber. Engineered wood beams may be used. All wood must be preservative-treated for use outdoors, or must be naturally durable wood. Number two grade or better is specified for all dimension lumber when building decks. Built-up beams should be assembled as shown in Figure 25.

Deck beam span distance may be determined using Table 4. Note that the span distances in Table 4 assume that the beam is supporting joists coming from one side of the deck. The beam depth should be at least as deep as the joist depth if the joists are supported at the beam by joist hangers.

Deck beams should be supported by a post, by another beam (engineering analysis may be required), or by a joist hanger. Deck beams should not be supported by a wood ledger, by angle brackets, or only by nails.

FIGURE 25: Deck Beam Assembly and Span Measurement

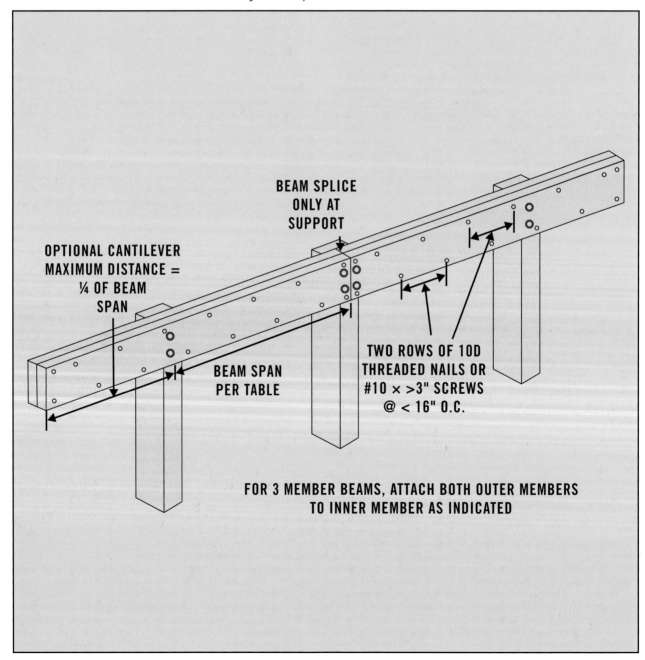

BEAM SPLICE ONLY AT SUPPORT

OPTIONAL CANTILEVER MAXIMUM DISTANCE = ¼ OF BEAM SPAN

BEAM SPAN PER TABLE

TWO ROWS OF 10D THREADED NAILS OR #10 × >3" SCREWS @ < 16" O.C.

FOR 3 MEMBER BEAMS, ATTACH BOTH OUTER MEMBERS TO INNER MEMBER AS INDICATED

TABLE 4: DECK BEAM MAXIMUM SPAN DISTANCE

WOOD SPECIES	BEAM SIZE	DECK JOIST SPAN DISTANCE LESS THAN OR EQUAL TO					
		6'	8'	10'	12'	14'	16'
Southern Pine	(2) 2 × 8	8'6"	7'4"	6'6"	5'11"	5'1"	4'9"
	(2) 2 × 10	10'1"	8'9"	7'9"	7'1"	6'6"	5'9"
	(2) 2 × 12	11'11"	10'4"	9'2"	8'4"	7'9"	7'3"
	(3) 2 × 8	10'7"	9'3"	8'3"	7'6"	6'11"	6'5"
	(3) 2 × 10	12'9"	11'0"	9'9"	8'9"	8'3"	7'8"
	(3) 2 × 12	15'0"	13'0"	11'7"	10'6"	9'9"	9'1"
Douglas Fir-Larch, Hem-Fir, Spruce-Pine-Fir	(2) 2 × 8	6'7"	5'8"	5'1"	4'7"	4'3"	3'10"
	(2) 2 × 10	8'1"	7'0"	6'3"	5'8"	5'3"	4'10"
	(2) 2 × 12	9'5"	8'2"	7'3"	6'7"	6'1"	5'8"
	(3) 2 × 8	9'5"	8'3"	7'4"	6'8"	6'2"	5'9"
	(3) 2 × 10	11'9"	10'2"	9'1"	8'3"	7'7"	7'1"
	(3) 2 × 12	13'8"	11'10"	106"	9'7"	8'10"	8'3"

In most cases it is far more economical to fabricate your own beams by laminating structured lumber, using exterior construction adhesive and nails for reinforcement.

FIGURE 26: Deck Beam Support on a Post

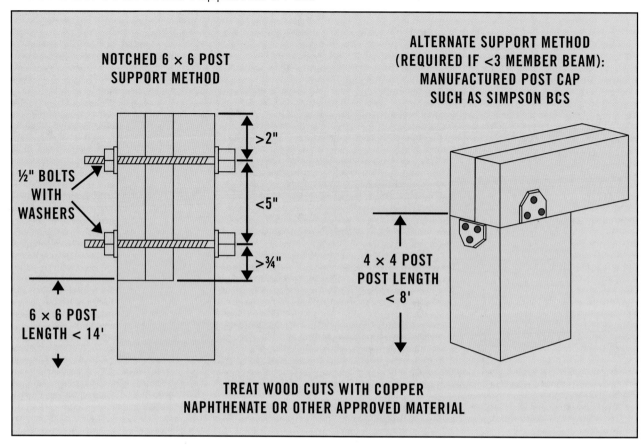

NOTCHED 6 × 6 POST
SUPPORT METHOD

½" BOLTS
WITH
WASHERS

>2"

<5"

>¾"

6 × 6 POST
LENGTH < 14'

ALTERNATE SUPPORT METHOD
(REQUIRED IF <3 MEMBER BEAM):
MANUFACTURED POST CAP
SUCH AS SIMPSON BCS

4 × 4 POST
POST LENGTH
< 8'

TREAT WOOD CUTS WITH COPPER
NAPHTHENATE OR OTHER APPROVED MATERIAL

A deck beam that is supported by a post should bear on the top of a post using one of the two methods shown in Figure 26. A deck beam should not be installed on the side of a post.

There are restrictions when another beam and a properly sized and installed joist hanger support a deck beam. Deck beam span distances in Table 4 do not include the load imposed by other beams. Table 4 (see page 83) may not be used when a beam supports another beam. Table 4 may be used when supporting trimmers used to frame around cantilevered projections.

Deck ledger attachment to the house as described in Chapter 5 does not include the load imposed by a beam or a trimmer. A joist hanger supporting a beam or a trimmer at the deck ledger should be bolted or screwed to the house rim joist according to the joist hanger manufacturer's instructions. These joist hangers are often special-order connectors.

SPOTTED IN THE FIELD

A deck beam should not be supported on the side of a post.

How Should Trimmers Around Cantilevered Projections Be Installed?

Deck ledgers that provide structural support for the deck may not be attached to cantilevered projections from the house. Common cantilevered projections include bay windows and framed fireplaces. These projections are not usually designed to bear the load imposed by the deck.

There are two options for dealing with cantilevered projections. One option is to make the deck freestanding at the projection. The other easier and more common option is to frame around the projection. Trimmers (beams) are installed on each side of the projection and a header (beam) is installed between the trimmers. Deck joists between the trimmers are attached to the header using appropriate joist hangers.

FIGURE 27: Framing Around Cantilevered Projections Using Trimmers and a Header

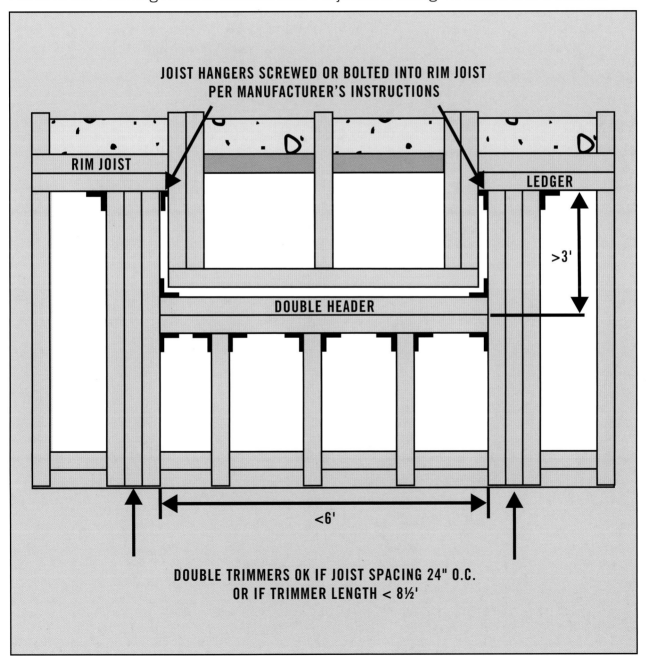

JOIST HANGERS SCREWED OR BOLTED INTO RIM JOIST
PER MANUFACTURER'S INSTRUCTIONS

RIM JOIST

LEDGER

>3'

DOUBLE HEADER

<6'

DOUBLE TRIMMERS OK IF JOIST SPACING 24" O.C.
OR IF TRIMMER LENGTH < 8½'

How Should Decking and the Rim Joist Be Installed?

Decking is another term for the floorboards on a deck. Decking is usually preservative-treated wood that is 2 × 4, 2 × 6, or 5/4 × 6. Larger size nominal two-inch-thick lumber may be used as decking, but these larger sizes tend to deform (usually cup) and may not last as long as smaller sizes.

Decking may be wood composite materials, plastic, and metal. Composite, plastic, and metal decking should be installed according to manufacturer's instructions. These instructions may include restrictions on how far the material may span between supports and on how close the material may be to soil.

Nominal two-inch-thick decking may span up to 24 inches between deck joist supports. Decking near the maximum span may deflect and feel spongy. Note that decking installed at an angle to the deck joists spans a greater distance than the deck joist on center spacing. Decking using 5/4 lumber is limited to 16 inches between deck joist supports.

Wood decking and the rim board should be installed as shown in Figure 28. Fasteners should be installed flush with the top of the decking. Fasteners that are driven into the decking form water pockets that will allow the wood around the fastener to deteriorate. This deterioration can cause loose decking and premature aging of the decking that requires decking replacement.

Manufactured wood decking, even when made of composite material, is not usually recommended for use at or near the soil.

FIGURE 28: Wood Decking and Rim Joist Installation

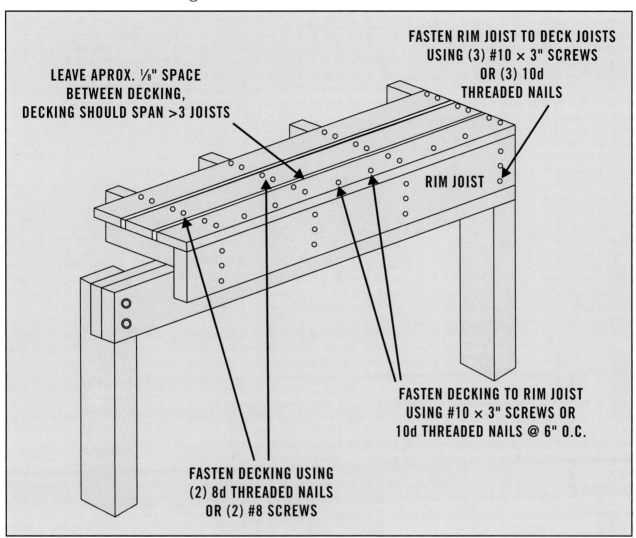

LEAVE APROX. ⅛" SPACE
BETWEEN DECKING,
DECKING SHOULD SPAN >3 JOISTS

FASTEN RIM JOIST TO DECK JOISTS
USING (3) #10 × 3" SCREWS
OR (3) 10d
THREADED NAILS

RIM JOIST

FASTEN DECKING TO RIM JOIST
USING #10 × 3" SCREWS OR
10d THREADED NAILS @ 6" O.C.

FASTEN DECKING USING
(2) 8d THREADED NAILS
OR (2) #8 SCREWS

Fasteners driven into decking can cause premature decking deterioration.

What Are Some Common Deck Framing Defects?

Common deck framing defects include the following:

1. Deck joists are too long between supports.

2. Deck joists and beams are extended too far (cantilevered) past supports.

3. Deck joists are not supported by a joist hanger.

4. Deck beam is too long between supports.

5. Deck beam is attached to the side of the deck post (beam is not supported on top of the post).

6. Joints between sections of built-up beams are not supported at a post.

7. Joist hangers, screws, and nails are not hot-dipped galvanized steel or stainless steel.

8. Deck framing components, fasteners, connectors, and joist hangers are damaged or deteriorated.

9. Deck joists are over-notched.

10. Deck materials that are not rated for ground contact are touching the soil, or are too near the soil.

11. Joist hangers are improperly installed (e.g., improper fasteners, all fasteners not installed, joist is set in joist hanger more than ⅛ inch from the beam or ledger).

12. Deck ledger is attached to a cantilevered projection.

What Should I Do If There Are Problems with My Deck Framing?

Correcting deck framing problems depends on the problem and on the age of the deck. If the deck is at or beyond the end of its service life, and if the problems are numerous or significant, it may be more cost effective, and safer, to remove the deck and start over. Significant defects include rusted and damaged fasteners, joist hangers, and connectors, and visibly deteriorated deck joists and beams.

A deck with minor defects that is still within its service life may be repairable. Replacing deteriorated decking may help extend the deck service life. Joist hangers can sometimes be added or replaced without too much difficulty.

If you are not sure about the best way to solve your deck framing problems, you should consult with a qualified engineer or home inspector to determine your best course of action. A qualified professional may find problems in addition to framing problems.

Many codes will allow you to simply toenail deck joists to beams where they cross, but a metal fastener (here, a hurricane tie) provides more resistance against joist movement.

Replacing some worn decking is not an especially difficult or even expensive deck repair. But if the structural framework is compromised, replacing the deck is usually the best bet. A few minor problems may be addressed by sistering a structural member to the affected member (right photo) but this should only be done on a very limited basis.

Chapter 9: Deck Posts, Footings, and Bracing

● ● ● ● ●

What Are Deck Posts, Footings, and Bracing?

A deck, by definition, is raised above the ground. Deck posts are the vertical structural components that support the deck above the ground. Decks that are supported at the house by a deck ledger have at least two posts. Many decks have three or more posts.

A footing transmits the load from the deck post to the soil. The soil is the actual load-bearing component, so it is important that the footing bear on solid, undisturbed soil. The bottom of the footing should be located below the local frost depth, or at least 12 inches below the soil level, whichever is deeper. A proper size footing should exist under every deck post, including posts that support hair stringers.

Bracing helps keep the deck from moving side to side. This side-to-side movement can weaken important connections between deck components. Weakened connections can result in deck failure.

Why Are Deck Posts, Footings, and Bracing Important?

As discussed in Chapter 3, a deck is a system. While it is uncommon to trace a deck failure directly to deck post, footing, and bracing installation defects, these defects can, over time, contribute to deck failure by placing stress on the deck system.

How Should Deck Posts Be Installed?

Deck posts are usually wood. Deck posts made from 6 × 6 Southern pine, Douglas fir, hem-fir, and spruce-pine-fir are limited to not more than 14 feet tall. Deck posts made from 4 × 4s of these wood species are limited to not more than eight feet tall. Other wood species and larger wood sizes may be used. Deck post height is measured from the top of the footing or from soil level (whichever is higher) to the bottom of the beam. Situations exist when the deck post height should be less than the maximum height. Refer to Table 5 (see page 96).

FIGURE 29: Maximum Bowing of a Deck Post   FIGURE 30: Maximum Deck Post Out of Plumb

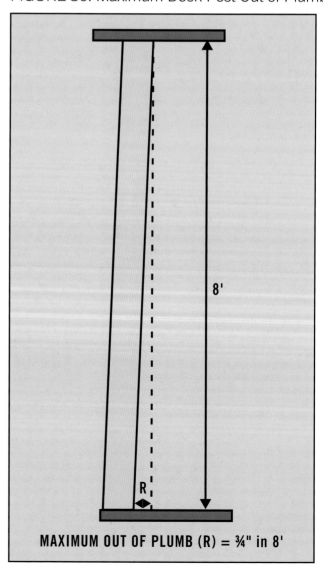

MAXIMUM BOW (B) = ¾" in 8'   **MAXIMUM OUT OF PLUMB (R) = ¾" in 8'**

Schedule 40 (a measure of steel thickness) or thicker steel pipe may be used as a deck post, with engineering approval. Steel should be covered with a rust-proof coating on both the inside and the outside of the pipe.

Wood deck posts should be free of significant defects. There should be no splits in the wood that run through the entire thickness of the wood. Openings between the wood fibers (surface checks) that do not run through the entire thickness of the wood are common in 4 × 4s and thicker wood and are usually not a concern. The deck post should be reasonably straight and plumb.

Deck posts that are rotted should be replaced. Rotted deck posts usually feel soft when probed with a sharp object, or are visibly deteriorated. Note, however, that sometimes a deck post will rot from the inside. This is especially common when a deck post is buried in the soil or is embedded in concrete. It can be difficult to detect a deck post that is rotted from the inside.

Bowed deck post.

SPOTTED IN THE FIELD

Deteriorated deck post.

The location of the deck post on its footing and the method of securing the deck post to the footing are important for structural stability. A deck post should be located near the center of the footing and should be secured to the footing using a post base. The top of footing should be above the soil when the deck post is secured to the footing using a post base or another approved method. Post bases are not intended for burial. A deck post may be embedded in a concrete footing, and the deck post may be located below the soil. This should be avoided if possible because the deck post is likely to deteriorate sooner.

All cuts in preservative-treated wood should be field-treated with a preservative such as copper naphthenate to reestablish the preservative treatment. This is especially important for deck post cuts. The cut end of deck posts are allowed to be embedded in concrete or installed in the soil if field-treated. This is not recommended.

SPOTTED IN THE FIELD

Deck post is off center on footing. Post base is rusted. Footing is too small.

How Should Deck Footings Be Installed?

Deck footings should be made from concrete that is poured into a proper size hole. Premanufactured concrete deck footing blocks, and other manufactured concrete products such as concrete masonry unit cap blocks, are not acceptable footings. The concrete should be at least 2,500-pound compressive strength; check the specifications on the concrete bag to verify the strength of the concrete.

The bottom of the footings should be at least 12 inches below the soil level, or below the local frost depth, whichever is deeper. The top of the footing may be above or below the soil level. Above the soil level is better because the deck post can be secured to the footing using a post base. A post base provides better resistance against post movement and helps the post last longer.

Deck footings, and the deck itself, should not be located where they will create problems. Decks should not be located above septic tanks, septic leach fields, wells, utility meters, fuel tanks, and any other component that may require access for service, filling, maintenance, or removal. Soil under the deck should slope away from the foundation at least six inches within the first 10 feet from the foundation.

Deck footings should be located at least five feet from the house. This is usually not a problem, except for free-standing decks. The bottom of footings closer than five feet from the house should be located at the same level as the house footings to avoid placing an unintended load on foundation walls.

FIGURE 31: Deck footings closer than 5' from the house should be at the house footing level.

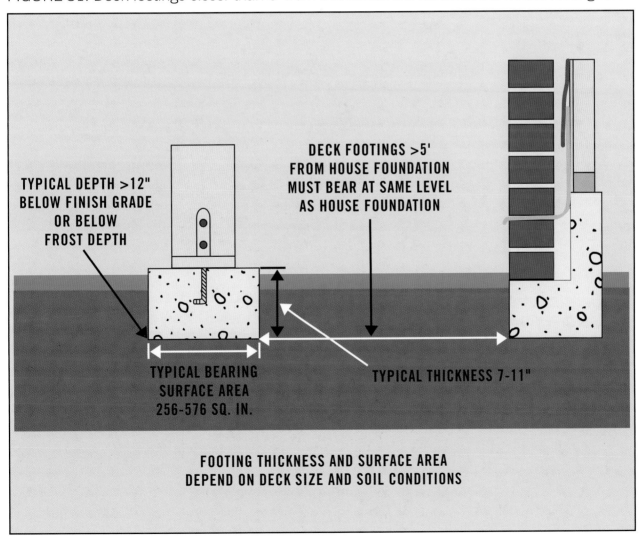

TYPICAL DEPTH >12" BELOW FINISH GRADE OR BELOW FROST DEPTH

DECK FOOTINGS >5' FROM HOUSE FOUNDATION MUST BEAR AT SAME LEVEL AS HOUSE FOUNDATION

TYPICAL BEARING SURFACE AREA 256-576 SQ. IN.

TYPICAL THICKNESS 7-11"

FOOTING THICKNESS AND SURFACE AREA DEPEND ON DECK SIZE AND SOIL CONDITIONS

Table 5 presents deck footing sizes for common combinations of deck beam spans and deck joist spans. Deck footing sizes in Table 5 are conservative and may be reduced in some cases. Refer to DCA 6-12 for information about reducing deck footing size.

TABLE 5: DECK POST HEIGHT AND FOOTING SIZES

BEAM SPAN	JOIST SPAN	MAXIMUM POST HEIGHT				MINIMUM FOOTING SIZE		
		SOUTHERN PINE	DOUGLAS FIR-LARCH	HEM-FIR	SPRUCE- PINE-FIR	ROUND FOOTING	SQUARE FOOTING	FOOTING THICKNESS
6'	≤ 10'	14'	14'	14'	14'	18"	16" × 16"	7"
	≤ 14'	14'	14'	14'	14'	21"	18" × 18"	8"
	≤ 18'	14'	14'	12'	11'	24"	21" × 21"	10"
8'	≤ 10'	14'	14'	14'	14'	20"	18" × 18"	8"
	≤ 14'	14'	14'	14'	11'	24"	21" × 21"	10"
10'	≤ 10'	14'	14'	14'	12'	23"	20" × 20"	9"
	≤ 14'	14'	13'	11'	8'	27"	24" × 24"	11"
	≤ 18'	12'	11'	8'	2'	31"	27" × 27"	13"
12'	≤ 10'	14'	14'	12'	10'	25"	22" × 22"	10"
	≤ 14'	13'	12'	9'	5'	30"	26" × 26"	13"
	≤ 18'	11'	9'	6'	2'	34"	30" × 30"	15"

FIGURE 32: Options for Installing Deck Footings and Posts

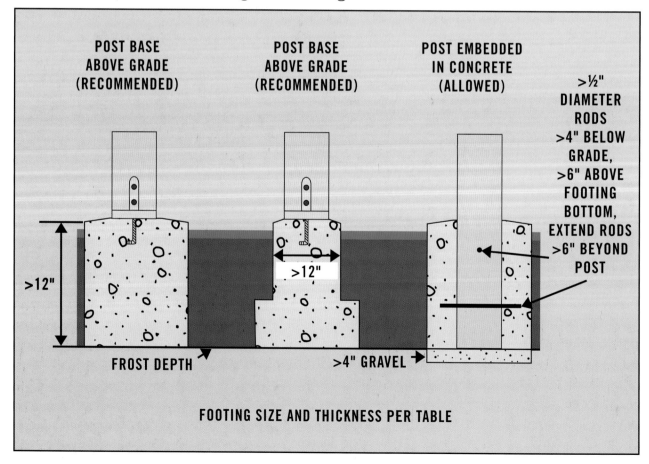

POST BASE ABOVE GRADE (RECOMMENDED)

POST BASE ABOVE GRADE (RECOMMENDED)

POST EMBEDDED IN CONCRETE (ALLOWED)

>½" DIAMETER RODS >4" BELOW GRADE, >6" ABOVE FOOTING BOTTOM, EXTEND RODS >6" BEYOND POST

>12"

>12"

FROST DEPTH

>4" GRAVEL

FOOTING SIZE AND THICKNESS PER TABLE

How Should Deck Bracing Be Installed?

Deck bracing should be installed between the corner deck posts and the deck beam. Deck bracing should not be attached to any interior deck posts. At least 2 × 4 lumber should be installed using ½-inch diameter screws with a washer on the head end. The brace should be about two feet beyond the post and about two feet below the beam.

Bracing between the post and beam on freestanding decks will reduce movement that can weaken the deck.

FIGURE 33: Deck Bracing

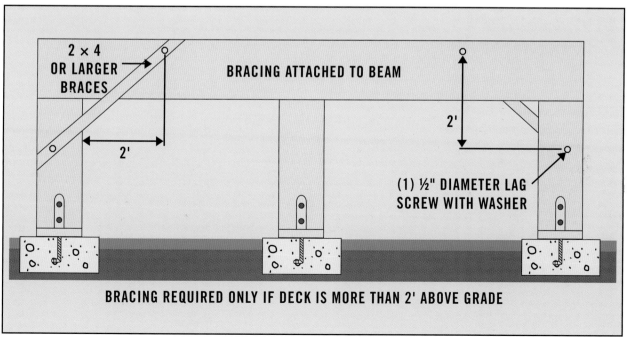

What Are Some Common Deck Post, Footing, and Bracing Defects?

Common deck post, footings, and bracing defects include the following:

1. Deck post is too tall for the post thickness and wood species.

2. Deck post is deteriorated or damaged.

3. Deck post is improperly secured, or is not secured, to the deck beam or to the deck footing.

4. Deck post is too far out of plumb.

5. Deck post is bowed.

6. Deck post is not centered on the deck footing.

7. Deck footing is too small or not thick enough.

8. Deck footing is not deep enough.

9. Deck footing is made from improper materials, such as concrete blocks.

10. Deck footing is close to the house, but the bottom of the footing is not at the house footing level.

11. Deck bracing is absent.

12. Deck bracing is improperly installed.

What Should I Do If There Are Problems with My Deck Post, Footings, or Bracing?

Substituting the correct deck post, post cap, post base, and deck footing for existing incorrect or deteriorated components usually involves raising the deck with a jack, removing the incorrect or deteriorated components, and adding new components. Raising the deck with a jack is very dangerous and requires skill, experience, and the right tools, especially if the deck is high above the ground. Unless you have advanced do-it-yourself skills and the right tools, you should consider having a qualified and insured contractor do this work.

Adding or repairing deck bracing is relatively easy, except for decks that are high above the ground. This is a moderate-level do-it-yourself project.

If you are not sure about the best way to solve your deck post, footings, and bracing problems, you should consult with a qualified contractor or home inspector to determine your best course of action.

A qualified professional may find problems in addition to these problems.

Residential Deck Inspection Checklist

General Deck Conditions

Structure Type

- ❏ Deck is attached to house.
  - Okay to use this checklist.

- ❏ Deck is freestanding.
  - Okay to use this checklist.

- ❏ Balcony is cantilevered, visible framing.
  - Do not use this checklist; recommend professional evaluation.

- ❏ Balcony is cantilevered, concealed framing.
  - Do not use this checklist; strongly recommend professional evaluation.

Structure Age
(If 20 years or more, recommend professional evaluation.)

Fasteners, Connectors & Hangers

- ❏ All fasteners, connectors, and hangers are recommended for outdoor use (look for a Z or SS in the connector model number).
  - If not, recommend replacing fasteners or connectors.

- ❏ Manufacturer-recommended fastener is installed in all round and obround connector and hanger holes.
  - If not, recommend fastener installation per manufacturer's instructions.

- ❏ Red rust is present on fasteners, connectors, or hangers.
  - Recommend replacing rusted components.

- ❏ Monitor fasteners, connectors, and hangers for red rust if white rust is present.

Special Conditions
(If yes, recommend professional evaluation of special conditions.)

- ❏ Heavy corrosion potential (1 mile from ocean).

- ❏ High wind potential (50 miles from ocean).

- ❏ Heavy loads (2' snow or more, spas, hot tubs, etc.).

- ❏ Earthquake potential.

- ❏ Deck is not a rectangle, or is multi-level.

- ❏ Deck supports a roof (e.g., a screened porch).

- ❏ House floor joists or trusses are parallel to attached deck ledger.

- ❏ House band board is not dimension lumber, or is 1"-thick or more manufactured rim joist.

- ❏ House floor structure is trusses.

- ❏ Deck is 1' or less, or more than 14' above ground.

- ❑ Deck ledger is attached to foundation (e.g., concrete block, concrete, brick).

- ❑ Deck ledger is attached to the house through wall covering (e.g., brick, siding).

Deck Ledger Attachment

- ❑ Deck ledger is not #2 grade or better, 2 × 8 or larger, preservative-treated Southern pine, douglas fir-larch, spruce pine fir, or hem fir.
  - Recommend professional evaluation.

- ❑ Lateral load connectors are not installed.
  - Strongly recommend installing these connectors.

- ❑ Deck ledger is attached to house using only nails.
  - Do not use deck. Strongly recommend professional evaluation.

- ❑ Deck ledger is detaching from house.
  - Do not use deck. Strongly recommend professional evaluation.

- ❑ Fasteners are not ½" diameter machine bolts with washers on both ends, or are not ½" diameter lag screws with washer on head end (screw penetrates house band board/rim joist).
  - Recommend installing fasteners per DCA 6-12, or fastener manufacturer's instructions.

- ❑ Fasteners are spaced more than 12" apart, or are not staggered vertically.
  - Recommend installing fasteners per DCA 6-12.

- ❑ Deck ledger is deteriorated, damaged, or soft, especially around fasteners.
  - Do not use deck. Strongly recommend professional evaluation.

Deck Flashing

- ❑ Aluminum flashing is present on decks built after 2004.
  - Recommend replacing flashing.

- ❑ No visible flashing is present.
  - Recommend professional evaluation.

- ❑ Flashing is incomplete or not fully visible.
  - Recommend monitoring inside house for water stains and damage.

- ❑ Flashing relies on fasteners, caulk, or sealants to maintain water-tightness.
  - Recommend monitoring inside house for water stains and damage.

- ❑ Flashing is rusted, corroded, or damaged.
  - Recommend replacing flashing.

- ❑ Water stain or damage is observed inside where deck is attached to house, or under door to deck.
  - Do not use deck if damage is significant. Recommend professional evaluation and repair.

Deck Guards and Stair Guards

- ❑ Guards are not installed on a deck that is more than 30" above ground.
  - Strongly recommend installing guards.

- ❑ Guards are less than 36" tall.
  - Recommend installing proper height guards.

- ❑ Guard posts are smaller than 4 × 4.
  - Recommend installing proper size guard posts.

- ❑ Guard posts are spaced more than 6' apart.
  - Recommend installing additional guard posts.

- ❑ Guard posts are notched.
  - Recommend replacing guard posts.

- ❑ Guard posts are attached using only nails.
  - Strongly recommend installing bolts and load connectors at all guard posts.

- ❑ Guard posts are not secured using load connectors.
  - Strongly recommend installing bolts and load connectors at all guard posts.

- ❑ Vertical components (e.g., balusters) allow a 4" diameter sphere to pass through (4⅜" for stair guards).
  - Recommend installing additional vertical components.

- ❏ Triangle formed by stair guard, riser, and tread allows a 6" diameter sphere to pass through.
  - Recommend installing additional vertical components.

- ❏ Guard posts, vertical components, or the boards to which they are attached are deteriorated, damaged, or soft, especially around fasteners or connectors.
  - Strongly recommend professional evaluation.

- ❏ Guards feel loose or unstable when pushing on them.
  - Strongly recommend professional evaluation.

Deck Stair Handrails

- ❏ Deck stair handrails are not graspable.
  - Recommend installing graspable handrails.

- ❏ Deck stair handrails are not continuous over a flight of stairs.
  - Recommend installing continuous handrails.

- ❏ Deck stair handrails do not terminate with a return or a newel.
  - Recommend installing a return or newel.

- ❏ Deck stair handrails feel loose or unstable when pushing on them.
  - Strongly recommend professional evaluation.

Deck Stair Stringers

- ❏ Deck stair stringers are not #2 grade or better, 2 × 12 or larger, preservative-treated Southern pine, douglas fir-larch, or hem fir.
  - Recommend professional evaluation.

- ❏ Deck stair stringer throat is less than 5".
  - Recommend installing additional support posts under stringers.

- ❏ Deck stair stringers are attached using nails that are withdrawing from where the stringers attach to the deck.
  - Do not use stairs. Strongly recommend professional evaluation.

- ❏ Deck stair stringers do not fully bear on the deck joist at the top of the stairs.
  - Do not use stairs. Strongly recommend professional evaluation.

- ❏ Deck stair stringers do not terminate at a solid landing, or are not properly supported, at the bottom of the stairs.
  - Recommend professional evaluation.

- ❏ Deck stair stringers do not have at least 1½ of bearing at the heel of the seat cut at the bottom of the stairs.
  - Recommend professional evaluation.

- ❏ Deck stair stringer span is more than 6' for cut stringers and 13' 3" for solid stringers.
  - Recommend installing additional support posts under stringers.

- ❏ Deck stair treads are less than 10" deep.
  - Recommend professional evaluation.

- ❏ Open risers between deck stair treads allow a 4" diameter sphere to pass through.
  - Recommend installing a riser closing component.

- ❏ Deck stair riser height difference is more than ⅜".
  - Recommend professional evaluation.

- ❏ Deck stair stringers or treads, or the boards to which they are attached, are deteriorated, damaged, or soft, especially around fasteners or connectors.
  - Do not use stairs. Strongly recommend professional evaluation.

- ❏ Deck stairs feel springy, wobbly, or unstable when walking on them.
  - Do not use stairs. Strongly recommend professional evaluation.

Deck Framing

❏ Deck floor joists are not #2 grade or better preservative-treated Southern pine, douglas fir-larch, or hem fir, or an approved naturally durable wood.
  - Recommend professional evaluation.

❏ Deck floor joists are supported only by nails (no joist hanger or 2 × 2 ledger strip).
  - Do not use deck. Strongly recommend professional evaluation.

❏ Deck floor joists are supported by a cantilevered structure.
  - Recommend professional evaluation.

❏ Deck floor joists are not fully seated in the joist hanger, or on the ledger strip.
  - Recommend professional evaluation. Do not use deck if joist movement is suspected.

❏ Deck floor joists are notched more than ¼ of the actual joist depth at the ends (measure to the saw kerf).
  - Recommend professional evaluation.

❏ Joints between deck beam members are not supported by a deck post.
  - Recommend installing a deck post and footing.

❏ Deck beam is supported on the side of the deck posts (not bearing on top of the posts).
  - Recommend installing beam attachment hardware.

❏ Deck framing (joists, beams, flooring) is deteriorated, damaged, or soft, especially around fasteners or connectors.
  - Strongly recommend professional evaluation.

❏ Deck feels springy, wobbly, or unstable when walking on it.
  - Do not use deck. Strongly recommend professional evaluation.

Deck Posts, Footing, Bracing

❏ 4 × 4 deck posts are more than 8' tall, or 6 × 6 deck posts are more than 14' tall.
  - Recommend professional evaluation.

❏ Deck posts are bowed, or are not plumb.
  - Recommend professional evaluation.

❏ Deck posts are not in the center of the footing.
  - Recommend professional evaluation.

❏ Deck posts are not attached to the footing, or are not attached to the deck.
  - Recommend installing attachment hardware.

❏ Deck footings are not poured concrete that are at least 18" diameter or at least 16 × 16" rectangular.
  - Recommend professional evaluation.

❏ Deck is not braced, or is not braced between end deck posts and beam (bracing is not required if deck is less than 2' above ground).
  - Recommend installing braces.

❏ Free-standing deck is not braced between end deck posts and deck rim joists (bracing is not required if deck is less than 2' above ground).
  - Recommend installing braces.

❏ Deck posts are deteriorated, damaged, or soft, especially around fasteners or connectors.
  - Do not use deck. Strongly recommend professional evaluation.

Appendix 1

Sample Deck Plans

Most of the successes and failures in deck building occur in the planning stage. In some cases, you may be working from an old plan that no longer reflects current codes. Or if you are using your own design and plan, you may have made a math error, misinterpreted a code, or simply forgot to include something. But whether you are using original plans or purchased plans, you will need to have working plan drawing to present to your municipal building department along with the other application materials. On the following pages, you'll see examples of deck plans for a first-story walkout deck and a second-story walkout deck. You may use them as a starter for your own project, or simply review them to get a sense of the kinds of views, lists, and information you will need to decide up front when submitting your own deck plan.

Ground Level Walkout Deck

Sometimes less really is more. This modest deck has a pleasing shape and is perched high enough to provide a clear view of the yard. Even better, the deck is a study in simplicity and it won't cost you a lot in either time or money. The framing and decking plans are straightforward and uncomplicated. You can likely build the entire structure over the course of two or three weekends, even if you have limited carpentry and building experience. That means that before a month is out, you'll have access to a convenient outdoor platform that can be used for a relaxing meal surrounded by nature, a place to read the paper, or to just sit and recharge your batteries after a long day at work.

This basic rectangular platform is as plainly handsome as it is useful and easy to build.

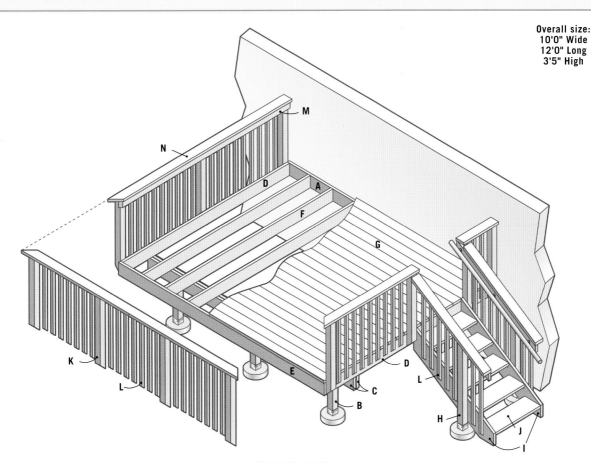

Overall size:
10'0" Wide
12'0" Long
3'5" High

SUPPLIES

18"-diameter footing forms (5)

J-bolts (5)

6 × 6" metal post base and fasteners (3)

4 × 4" metal post base and fasteners (2)

6 × 6" metal post caps and fasteners (3)

2 × 8" joist hangers and fasteners (18)

2 × 8" joist hangers concealed flange (2)

Tread angles and fasteners (10)

Adjustable stair stringer connectors (2)

DTT1 lateral load connectors (4)

Simpson DTT2 connectors and fasteners (14)

½" × 7" galvanized machine bolts, nuts,
   and washers (14)#10 × 3" galvanized
   deck screws

16d galvanized threaded shank nails

#8 × 2½" galvanized deck screws

⅜ × 4" lag screws and washers (20)

½" × 5" lag screws and washers (11)

¼ × 1¼" lag screws and washers (80)

4½ × 5" galvanized lag screws and washers

Peel-and-stick membrane flashing (13')

Galvanized steel L flashing (13')

Exterior silicone caulk (3 tubes)

Concrete as needed

Treated handrail

Handrail brackets (2)

2 × 4 × 8-point 2 × 4

LUMBER LIST

QTY.	SIZE	MATERIAL	PART
4	2 × 8" × 12'	Trtd. lumber	Ledger (A), Beam bds (C), Rim joist (E)
1	6 × 6" × 8'	Trtd. lumber	Deck posts (B)
10	2 × 8" × 10'	Trtd. lumber	End joists (D), Joists (F)
25	2 × 6" × 12'	Trtd. lumber	Decking (G), Rail cap (N)
7	4 × 4" × 8'	Trtd. lumber	Stair posts (H), Rail posts (K)
2	2 × 12" × 8'	Trtd. lumber	Stringers (I)
3	2 × 12" × 6'	Trtd. lumber	Treads (J)
32	2 × 2" × 8'	Trtd. lumber	Balusters (L)
2	2 × 4" × 12'	Trtd. lumber	Top rail (M)
2	2 × 4" × 10'	Trtd. lumber	Top rail (N)

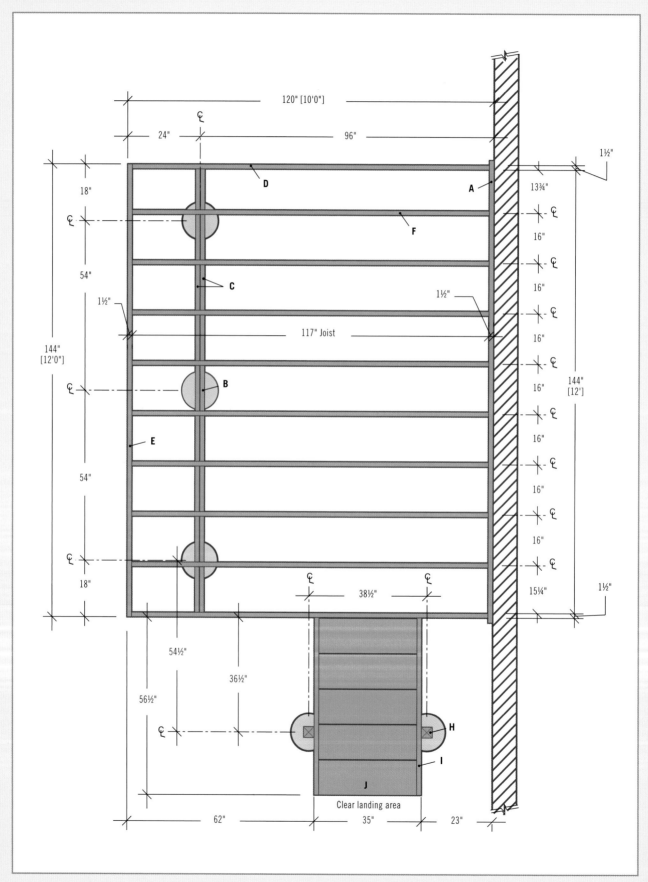

120" [10'0"]

24"   96"

1½"

13¾"

18"   D   A

54"   F

16"

1½"   C   16"

1½"

117" Joist   16"

144"
[12'0"]   16"

B   144"
[12']

16"

E

54"   16"

16"

18"   15¼"   1½"

38½"

54½"

36½"   H

56½"   I

J

Clear landing area

62"   35"   23"

⚙ ELEVATION

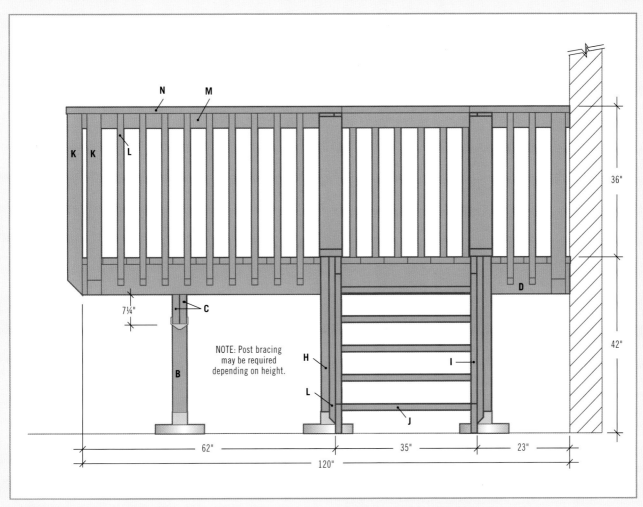

N
M
K K
L
36"
42"
7¼"
C
B
NOTE: Post bracing
may be required
depending on height.
H
I
L
J
D
62"
35"
23"
120"

⚙ STAIRWAY DETAIL

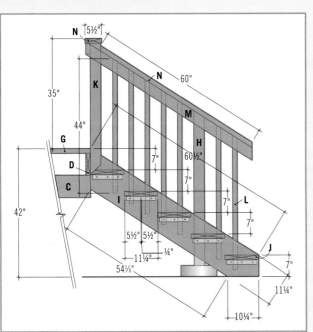

N 5½"
K
N 60"
35"
44"
M
G
H
D
7"
C
60½"
7"
I
7"
L
7"
5½" 5½"
¼"
11¼"
J
7"
54⅜"
11¼"
10¼"
42"

⚙ RAILING DETAIL

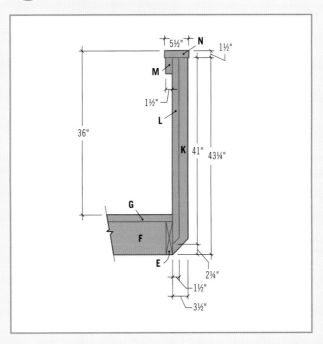

5½" N
1½"
M
1½"
L
36"
K 41" 43¼"
G
F
E
2¼"
1½"
3½"

Second-Story Walkout Deck

This simple rectangular deck provides a secure, convenient outdoor living space. The absence of a stairway prevents children from wandering away or unexpected visitors from wandering in. It also makes the deck easier to build.

Imagine how handy it will be to have this additional living area only a step away from your dining room or living room, with no more need to walk downstairs for outdoor entertaining, dining, or relaxing.

And if you'd like to add a stairway, just refer to Chapter 6 on stair-building (see page 52).

Simplicity, security, and convenience are the hallmarks of this elevated deck.

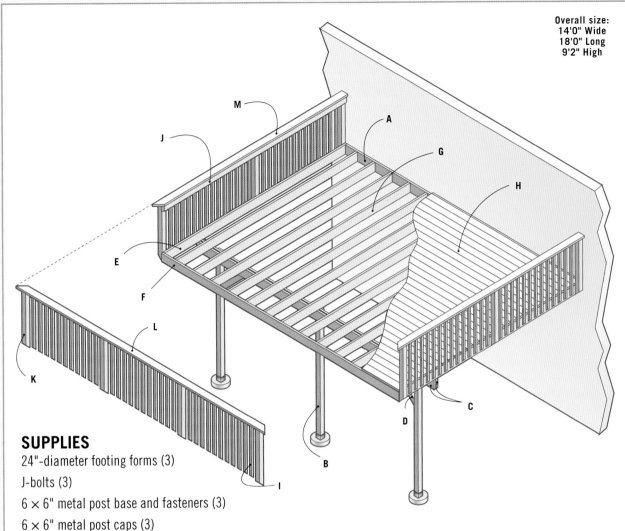

Overall size:
14'0" Wide
18'0" Long
9'2" High

SUPPLIES

24"-diameter footing forms (3)

J-bolts (3)

6 × 6" metal post base and fasteners (3)

6 × 6" metal post caps (3)

2 × 10" joist hangers and fasteners (28)

2 × 10" joist hangers concealed flange (2)

½ × 4" lag screws and washers (28)

½ × 5" lag screws and washers (23)

½ × 7" lag bolts, washers, and nuts (6)

Galvanized deck screws (#8 × 2½"; #10 × 3")

Simpson DTT1 lateral load connectors and fasteners (4)

Simpson DTT2 connectors and fasteners (16)

½" × 6" galvanized machine bolts, nuts, and washers (16)

16d galvanized threaded nails

Peel-and-stick membrane flashing (19')

Galvanized steel L flashing (19')

Metal flashing (18')

Silicone caulk (3 tubes)

Concrete as required

LUMBER LIST

QTY.	SIZE	MATERIAL	PART
2	2 × 12" × 20'	Trtd. lumber	Beam boards (C)
2	2 × 10" × 18'	Trtd. lumber	Ledger (A), Rim joist (F)
15	2 × 10" × 14'	Trtd. lumber	Joists (G), End joists (E)
3	6 × 6" × 10'	Trtd. lumber	Deck posts (B)
1	2 × 4" × 8'	Trtd. lumber	Braces (D)
32	2 × 6" × 18'	Trtd. lumber	Decking (H)
2	2 × 6" × 16'	Trtd. lumber	Top rail (J)
50	2 × 2" × 8'	Trtd. lumber	Balusters (I)
5	4 × 4" × 8'	Trtd. lumber	Rail posts (K)
1	2 × 6" × 16'	Trtd. lumber	Rail caps (L)
2	2 × 6" × 10'	Trtd. lumber	Rail caps (M)

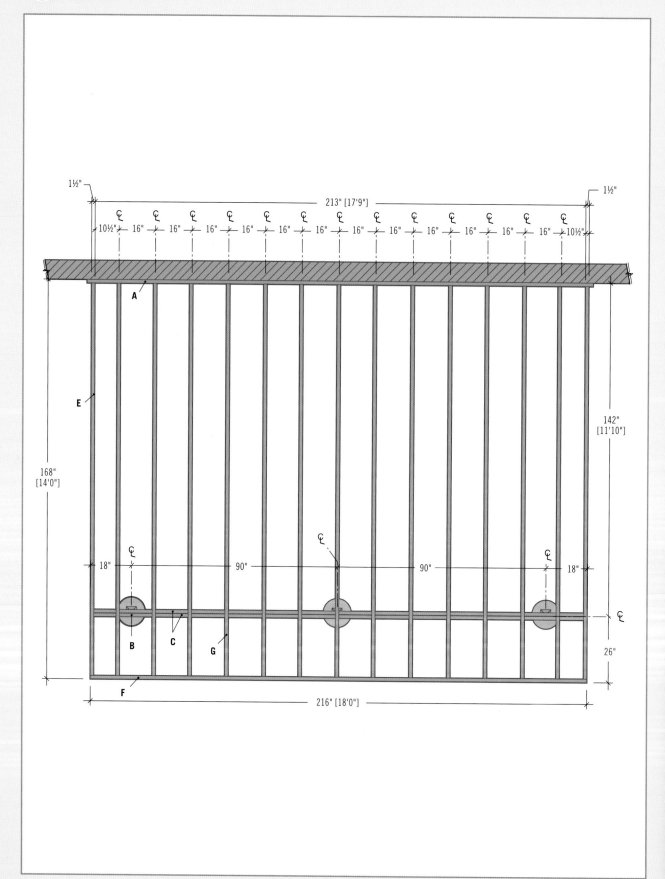

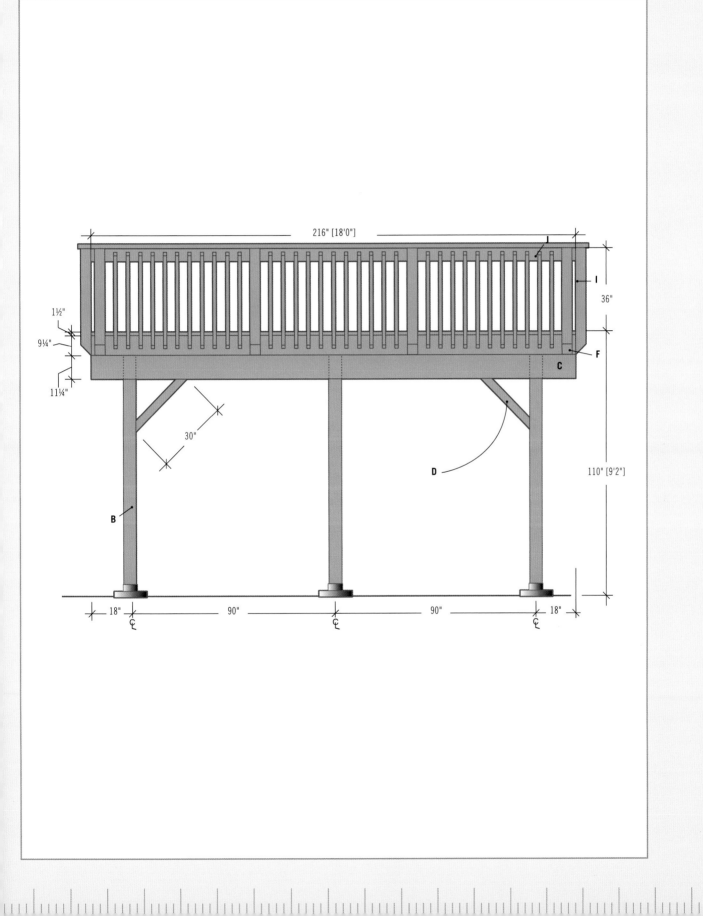

Appendix 2

Tips for Working with Deck Contractors

Good contractors are a little like hen's teeth. Often it seems as though there are not any. Good contractors *are* out there; the problem is finding them. Nothing you do guarantees that the contractor you hire will be a good one, and even good ones can do bad jobs. The following are some steps that will help improve the chance of finding, and successfully working with, a good contactor. For the sake of this discussion, we will assume that good contractors are also qualified contractors. This is usually true.

Check Out the Contractor

The first step in finding a good contractor is verifying the contractor's essential credentials.

1. Verify the contractor's license. Most states require contractors to be licensed and most states have websites where you can verify the contractor's license. You can often find information about complaints filed against the contractor at this site. Only use licensed contractors. A license is not a guarantee of a good contractor, but the lack of a license is often a sign of a bad contractor.

2. Obtain the contractor's certificate of insurance. A good contractor will be happy to provide a certificate from his/her insurance company, thus making it easy for the homeowner to verify with the insurance company. (Because from time to time, the information provided is outdated or perhaps does not exist, the homeowner should verify the contractor's insurance coverage.) The ideal contractor has general liability and workman's compensation insurance. General liability protects you in case the contractor damages something. Workman's compensation protects you in case a worker is injured while on your property. Yes, you could be sued by a worker injured on your property. Workman's compensation insurance is very expensive and not all contractors carry it. Not having general liability and workman's compensation isn't a deal breaker, but it is a risk consideration. Also, check what coverage your homeowner's insurance policy might provide if a worker is injured while on your property.

3. Check references, but not only those the contractor gives you. Check sites like Yelp and enter the contractor into a search engine such as Google.

Define the Scope of Work

A written scope of work definition is one of the best ways to avoid misunderstandings and the disasters that often follow. Be as precise as possible, but make allowances for the size of the job. A simple scope definition is appropriate for a simple job.

1. Identify products and materials to be used. For example, products and materials used to build a deck would include the types and sizes of lumber and other structural materials, the types of fasteners and other hardware such as joist hangers, and the types of flashing.

2. Identify the important work tasks to be performed. For example, a work task to build a deck would include producing a plan showing all details necessary to obtain a building permit, obtaining the building permit, removing and disposing of any existing deck, and removing and disposing of construction debris.

3. Specify that the contractor will perform all work in strict compliance with all building codes and will follow the manufacturer's instructions. This should occur regardless, but it helps to have it in writing.

4. Specify that the work will be performed under a building permit, if required in your jurisdiction. This should occur regardless, but it helps to have it in writing. Be very concerned if a contractor does not want to perform the work under a building permit. Do not let the contractor start work without a building permit in hand. Keep evidence of approved inspections in your records; it will help to have this when you sell your house.

Define the Payment Schedule

The complexity of the payment schedule depends on the complexity of the work. Small projects may have two or three payments. Large projects may have several progress payments. Typical payments include some amount upon signing of an agreement, progress payments, and the final payment.

1. Pay not more than 10 percent of the total contract price upon signing the agreement for the job. If materials need to be special ordered, this number may increase as reasonably necessary to pay for these materials. Rarely should the initial payment exceed 25 percent. (If the contractor asks for a large percentage, this may be a bad sign. Also, if the contractor asks for an advance, especially long before the start date, this may be a bad sign.)

2. Tie progress payments to completion of specific work tasks. For example, removing and disposing of an existing deck might be worth 20 percent.

3. Make a final payment of 10 to 25 percent when all work is completed according to the written agreement, including passing the building department inspection.

Define a Change Order Procedure (and Stick to It)

Expect the unexpected during home improvement projects, especially large deck building projects. Changes to the scope of work should only be made with a written agreement that describes the scope change and the price change. You and the contractor should sign the change order agreement. It is tempting to ignore change orders during the crunch of a project deadline, but both you and the contractor do so at your peril. Lack of written change orders causes more disagreements between contractors and customers than almost any other problem.

Contractor Red Flags

Ask for and read the contractor's contract during the initial negotiations. Here are a few red flags to watch for. These are not necessarily deal breakers, but they are a cause for concern.

1. Large up-front payments. It is reasonable for a contractor to ask for some money up front, especially if special-order materials are involved. Not including special-order materials, more than about 20 percent up front may be questionable.

2. Mandatory arbitration. Arbitration can be a good way to resolve disputes, and is not necessarily a problem. Realize, however, that arbitration is not free. You may be required to pay a non-refundable fee up front to initiate arbitration. If an arbiter, such as the American Arbitration Association, is specified in the contract, verify with the arbiter that the contractor is registered with the arbiter. Registration and arbiter review of the contractor's contract may be necessary before the arbiter will accept the dispute.

3. Social media ban. A contract clause that restricts your right to post negative comments about the contractor on social media is a major red flag. Almost all contractors have some dissatisfied clients, and some of those clients may be unreasonable. Attempting to restrict access to social media is not the best way to deal with clients, even unreasonable ones.

4. Legal cost shifting. The general rule is that each party pays its own legal/arbitration costs. A clause that makes you pay the contractor's legal/arbitration costs is a major red flag, unless the clause applies to both parties. It is more reasonable, though not ideal, to have a clause that obligates the loser in a dispute to pay the winner's legal/arbitration costs.

The Bottom Line

It is said that if you do not know where you are going, any road will take you there. Proper planning and a good written agreement will help you and your contractor arrive at your destination.

APPENDIX 3

Major Deck and Balcony Failures in the News, 2001–2016

NOTE: The data reported were not collected as part of a formal study and reflect only a sample of injuries and fatalities that were widely publicized by media sources. An analysis prepared for the Associated Press by the Consumer Product Safety Commission estimated that some 4,600 emergency room visits were associated with deck collapses, and another 1,900 with porch failures.

www.usnews.com/news/us/articles/2015/06/18/review-shows-deaths-seldom-occur-in-balcony-collapses

The table, Major Deck and Balcony Failures in the News 2001–2016, was compiled by Frank Woeste and Bruce A. Barker.

Atlanta, GA	DEC 2016	2 injured
Manchester, NH	NOV 2016	1 injured
Honolulu, HI	OCT 2016	1 injured, 1 fatality
Topsfield, MA	OCT 2016	1 injured
Birmingham, AL	SEP 2016	5 injured
Crownsville, MD	SEP 2016	2 injured
Halifax, NS	SEP 2016	1 injured
Hartford, CT	SEP 2016	31 injured
Mechanicsburg, PA	SEP 2016	7 injured
Medford, OR	SEP 2016	* injured
Millersville, MD	SEP 2016	2 injured
New London, CT	SEP 2016	1 injured
Colorado Springs, CO	AUG 2016	1 injured
Kalispell, MT	AUG 2016	11 injured
Sitka, AK	AUG 2016	10 injured
Lakeside, MT	AUG 2016	11 injured
Long Beach, NY	AUG 2016	* injured
Pikesville, MD	AUG 2016	4 injured
Setauket, NY	AUG 2016	2 injured
Suffolk, NY	AUG 2016	2 injured
Westminster, MA	AUG 2016	1 injured
Attleboro, RI	JUL 2016	3 injured

Chestnut Ridge, NY	JUL 2016	4 injured
Edgartown, MA	JUL 2016	8 injured
Halifax, NS	JUL 2016	6 injured
Lowell, MA	JUL 2016	2 injured
Paducah, KY	JUL 2016	4 injured
Peoria, IL	JUL 2016	1 fatality
Salvo, NC	JUL 2016	3 injured
Westphal, CA	JUL 2016	* injured
White Rock, BC	JUL 2016	2 injured
Wonder Lake, IL	JUL 2016	4 injured
Augusta, GA	JUN 2016	1 injured
Bridgewater, NJ	JUN 2016	2 injured
Brooklyn, NY	JUN 2016	16 injured
Corner Brook, CA	JUN 2016	3 injured
Erie, PA	JUN 2016	4 injured
North River, NL	JUN 2016	8 injured
Pennsauken, NJ	JUN 2016	1 injured
Rockville, MD	JUN 2016	2 injured
Sikeston, MO	JUN 2016	16 injured
Tulsa, OK	JUN 2016	2 injured
Vero Beach, FL	JUN 2016	* injured
Albany, NY	MAY 2016	2 injured
Atlanta, GA	MAY 2016	4 injured
Beaufort, NC	MAY 2016	0 injured
Chicago, IL	MAY 2016	1 injured
East Greenbush, NY	MAY 2016	2 injured
Marathon Township, MI	MAY 2016	10 injured
Pocatello, ID	MAY 2016	2 injured
Cedarville, OH	APR 2016	8 injured
Clemson, SC	APR 2016	4 injured
Gallagher Township, PA	APR 2016	13 injured
Portland, ME	APR 2016	1 fatality
Clifton, NJ	MAR 2016	0 injured
Frostburg, MD	MAR 2016	5 injured
Waterloo, ON	MAR 2016	2 injured
Bessemer, AL	FEB 2016	6 injured
Philadelphia, PA	FEB 2016	1 injured
Soulard, MO	FEB 2016	5 injured
Surrey, BC	FEB 2016	1 injured
Port Vue, PA	JAN 2016	1 injured
Danbury, CT	DEC 2015	2 injured
Elkton, MD	DEC 2015	4 injured
Evans, GA	NOV 2015	0 injured
Grand Rapids, MI	AUG 2015	1 injured

Burtonsville, MD	AUG 2015	2 injured
Emerald Isle, NC	AUG 2015	9 injured
Brome Lake, CA	AUG 2015	0 injuries
Columbia, MD	JUL 2015	5 injured
Omaha, NE	JUL 2015	2 injured
Rockland County, NY	JUL 2015	2 injured
Greely, CO	JUL 2015	7 injured
New Bedford, MA	JUL 2015	3 injured
Folsom, CA	JUL 2015	1 fatality
Lehi, UT	JUL 2015	4 injured
Emerald Isle, NC	JUL 2015	24 injured
Berkeley, CA	JUN 2015	7 injured, 6 fatalities
Yarmouth, NS	JUN 2015	12 injured
Cole Harbour, NS	JUN 2015	1 injured
Ottawa, ON	JUN 2015	1 injured
Pittsburgh, PA	JUN 2015	4 injured
Sitka, AK	JUN 2015	2 injured
Evanston, IL	MAY 2015	* injured
Noblesville, IN	MAY 2015	2 injured
Lithonia, GA	MAY 2015	9 injured
Cedarville, OH	APR 2015	8 injured
Fort Wayne, IN	APR 2015	2 injured
Portland, ME	APR 2015	1 fatality
Northampton, MA	APR 2015	1 injured
Knoxville, TN	APR 2015	1 injured
Beverly, MA	APR 2015	1 injured
Hingham, MA	FEB 2015	* injured
San Francisco, CA	JAN 2015	3 injured
Greenville, SC	NOV 2014	22 injured
Halifax, NS	SEP 2014	6 injured
Oakland, CA	SEP 2014	9 injured
Towson, MD	SEP 2014	7 injured
Ellenwood, GA	SEP 2014	6 injured
Philadelphia, PA	AUG 2014	1 injured
Clinton, TN	AUG 2014	1 injured
Atlanta, GA	AUG 2014	5 injured
Valley, NE	JUL 2014	2 injured
Chicago, IL	JUL 2014	1 injured
Folsom, CA	JUL 2014	0 injured
Penn Forest Township, PA	JUL 2014	6 injured
Ponte Vedra Beach, FL	JUN 2014	4 injured
Duluth, MN	JUN 2014	0 injured
Staten Island, NY	JUN 2014	1 injured
Pawleys Island, SC	JUN 2014	13 injured

Stone Mountain, GA	MAY 2014	13 injured
Stone Harbor, NJ	APR 2014	3 injured
Lynchburg, VA	JAN 2014	1 injured, 1 fatality
Philadelphia, PA	JAN 2014	2 injured, 1 fatality
New Albany, IN	DEC 2013	22 injured
Chico, CA	OCT 2013	14 injured
Winona, MN	OCT 2013	8 injured
Concord Township, DE	SEP 2013	7 injured
Dartmouth, NS	SEP 2013	15 injured
Ocean Isle Beach, NC	JUL 2013	21 injured
Champlin, MN	JUL 2013	4 injured
Miami, FL	JUN 2013	33 injured
Chicago, IL	JUN 2013	1 injured
Long Beach, NY	JUN 2013	5 injured
Wildwood, IL	MAY 2013	3 injured
Montgomery, AL	MAY 2013	* injured
Santa Barbara, CA	APR 2013	5 injured
Gulf Shores, AL	MAR 2013	7 injured
Montgomery, AL	DEC 2012	2 injured
Tallahassee, FL	OCT 2012	* injured
Powder Springs, GA	SEP 2012	1 injured
Louisville, KY	JUL 2012	4 injured
Austin, TX	JUL 2012	10 injured
Littleton, CO	JUL 2012	4 injured
Atlanta, GA	MAY 2012	7 injured
Ashland, NH	MAY 2012	* injured
Churubusco, IN	MAY 2012	* injured
Parkland, WA	FEB 2012	5 injured, 1 fatality
Melrose, MA	OCT 2011	1 fatality
Charlottesville, VA	SEP 2011	2 injured
Trappe, PA	SEP 2011	3 injured
Castleton, VT	SEP 2011	* injured
Golden, CO	AUG 2011	12 injured
Jefferson, CO	AUG 2011	4 injured
Philadelphia, PA	SEP 2010	7 injured
Austin, TX	AUG 2010	23 injured
Marietta, GA	JUL 2010	8 injured
Holden Beach, NC	JUN 2010	7 injured
Kingstowne, VA	JUN 2010	10 injured
Lexington, VA	MAY 2010	22 injured
Ocean Isle Beach, NC	JUL 2009	21 injured
Lawrenceville, GA	JUN 2009	4 injured
Wildwood, MO	JUN 2009	9 injured
Cary, IL	MAY 2009	2 injured

Richmond, VA	NOV 2008	20 injured
Vancouver, BC	OCT 2008	3 injured
Houston, TX	JUN 2008	1 injured, 2 fatalities
Ottawa, ON	JUN 2008	6 injured
Narragansett, ME	JAN 2008	10 injured
Wildwood, NJ	SEP 2007	* injured
Ship Bottom, NJ	JUL 2007	7 injured
Vancouver, BC	JUL 2007	2 injured
Oxford, CT	JUL 2007	4 injured
Harvey Cedars, NJ	JUL 2007	7 injured
Cape May, NJ	JUL 2007	9 injured
Warwick, RI	JUN 2007	5 injured
Fall River, KS	MAY 2007	* injured, 1 fatality
Norman, IL	MAY 2007	6 injured
Brooklyn, MD	MAR 2007	4 injured
Smithtown, NY	MAR 2007	7 injured
Melville, NY	JAN 2007	3 injured
Lawrenceville, GA	SEP 2006	4 injured
Concord, MA	SEP 2006	6 injured
Arlington, PA	AUG 2006	3 injured
Westerly, RI	AUG 2006	9 injured
Fitchburg, MA	AUG 2006	1 injured
Point Pleasant Beach, NJ	JUL 2006	6 injured
Needham, MA	JUL 2006	2 injured
Howells, NY	JUL 2006	15 injured
Covington, KY	JUL 2006	1 injured
Upper Marlboro, MD	JUN 2006	5 injured
Patterson, NY	JUN 2006	1 injured
Kripplebush, NY	JUN 2006	13 injured
Chesterfield, VA	JUN 2006	4 injured
McGaheysville, VA	JUN 2006	3 injured
Fitchburg, MA	JUN 2006	1 injured
Philadelphia, PA	JUN 2006	7 injured
Marietta, GA	MAY 2006	3 injured
Kitchener, ON	MAY 2006	2 injured
Chattanooga, TN	MAY 2006	2 injured
Annapolis, MD	JAN 2006	5 injured
Chicago, IL	DEC 2005	2 injured
Loveland, OH	OCT 2005	13 injured
Virginia Beach, VA	OCT 2005	33 injured
Seneca, SC	SEP 2005	7 injured
Elm Grove, WI	SEP 2005	9 injured

Minneapolis, MN	SEP 2005	3 injured
Arlington Heights, IL	AUG 2005	6 injured
Portland, OR	AUG 2005	10 injured
Sherwood, AR	AUG 2005	12 injured
Troy, IL	JUL 2005	7 injured
Fort Kent, ME	JUL 2005	5 injured
San Francisco, CA	JUN 2005	3 injured
Lincoln Park, IL	JUN 2005	2 injured
Allentown, PA	JUN 2005	2 injured
Charlottesville, VA	APR 2005	1 injured
Napa, CA	APR 2005	11 injured
Durham, NC	MAR 2005	3 injured
Columbus, OH	NOV 2004	1 fatality
Pierce County, WA	OCT 2004	7 injured, 1 fatality
Wilmington, NC	OCT 2004	8 injured
Milford, CT	SEP 2004	8 injured
St. Louis, MO	AUG 2004	2 injured
Polson, MT	JUL 2004	80 injured
Chicago, IL	JUN 2004	1 fatality
Elyria, OH	JUN 2004	6 injured
Victoria, BC	MAY 2004	10 injured
Tybee Island, GA	MAR 2004	* injured
Highlands, NJ	FEB 2004	7 injured
Charlottesville, VA	DEC 2003	1 injured, 1 fatality
Chilmark, MA	AUG 2003	10 injured
Queens, NY	AUG 2003	2 injured, 1 fatality
Tybee Island, GA	JUL 2003	9 injured, 1 fatality
Chula Vista, AL	JUN 2003	23 injured
Chicago, IL	JUN 2003	57 injured, 13 fatalities
Huntington, WV	MAY 2003	17 injured
Exton, PA	SEP 2002	11 injured
Egg Harbor, NJ	JUL 2002	4 injured
Point Pleasant, NJ	JUL 2002	33 injured
Wildwood, NJ	JUL 2002	10 injured
San Francisco, CA	NOV 2001	1 injured
Sea Isle City, NJ	AUG 2001	11 injured
Emerald Isle, NC	JUL 2001	* injured
Buffalo Grove, IL	JUN 2001	3 injured
Ossining, NY	JUN 2001	19 injured
Quincy, MA	MAY 2001	5 injured
Parkland, WA	FEB 2001	5 injured, 1 fatality

* = actual number not reported

References

American Wood Council 2013. Prescriptive Residential Wood Deck Construction Guide Based on the 2012 International Residential Code (DCA6-12 2013 Edition).

Anderson, Cheryl, Dr. Frank Woeste, and Dr. Joseph Loferski, Manual for the Inspection of Residential Wood Decks and Balconies. Madison, WI: Forest Products Society in cooperation with the International Code Council, 2003.

Barker, Bruce A. Everybody's Building Code. Cary, NC: Dream Home Consultants, LLC, 2015.

Bender, Don. Weyerhaeuser Professor, Washington State University. Personal communication. April 2015.

Bouldin, John. Virginia Tech University. Personal communication. March 2015.

International Code Council. 2015 International Residential Code for One- and Two-family Dwellings. Country Club Hills, IL: International Code Council, Inc., 2014.

Loferski, Joseph, and Frank Woeste, P.E, with Dustin Albright and Ricky Caudill. "Strong Rail-Post Connections for Wooden Decks," Journal of Light Construction, February 2005.

West, Anne W. "Deck Inspections: A matter of life and death," reprinted in the ASHI Reporter, July 2007.

Woeste, Frank 2008. "Coastal Resources: Safe and Durable Coastal Decks," Journal of Light Construction, March 2008.

Woeste, Frank. Virginia Tech University. Personal communication. April 2015.

Resources

American Society of Home Inspectors (ASHI)
Deck inspections and consultations
(847) 759-2820
www.homeinspector.org

American Wood Council
Deck construction guidelines (DCA 6-12)
(202) 463-2766
www.awc.org/codes-standards/publications/
dca6

Coastal Deck Construction Issues
*Structural Safety of Wood Decks and Deck
Guards*
The Construction Specifier, November 2013,
Loferski, Woeste
www.constructionspecifier.com/structural-
safety-of-wood-decks-and-deck-guards

Corrosion and Wood Preservative Treatments
*Preservatively Treated (PT) Lumber
Inspector Journal, Fall 2015*, Skip Walker
www.creia.org/assets/2.%20creia_ij_fall2015.
pdf

Deck Post Connections
*Strong Rail-Post Connections for Wooden Decks
Journal of Light Construction,* February
2005, Loferski, Woeste, et. al.
www.jlconline.com/how-to/framing/strong-
rail-post-connections-for-wooden-decks_o

FastenMaster
LedgerLok deck ledger screws
(800) 518-3569
www.fastenmaster.com/products/ledgerlok-
ledger-board-fastener.html

International Code Council
Deck construction code (International
Residential Code)
(888) 422-7233
www.iccsafe.org

North American Deck and Railing
Deck inspections and consultations,
inspection checklist
(215) 679-4884
www.nadra.org

Simpson Strong-Tie
Deck connectors, joist hangers, hardware
(800) 999-5099
www.strongtie.com/products/deckcenter

USP Structural Connectors
Deck connectors, joist hangers, hardware
(800) 328-5934
www.uspconnectors.com/us/products/
connectors/deck-fences

Wood Preservative Treatment
Specification Guide for Wolmanized®
Pressure-Treated Wood
www.buildingproductsplus.com/wp-content/
uploads/images/treated_wood_specguide.
pdf

Photo Credits

Bruce Bennett/Getty Images: 19

Simpson Strong-Tie: 49

Shutterstock: 4, 11, 13, 14, 15, 53, 65, 77

Metric Conversions

ENGLISH TO METRIC

TO CONVERT:	TO:	MULTIPLY BY:
Inches	Millimeters	25.4
Inches	Centimeters	2.54
Feet	Meters	0.305
Yards	Meters	0.914
Square inches	Square centimeters	6.45
Square feet	Square meters	0.093
Square yards	Square meters	0.836
Ounces	Milliliters	30.0
Pints (US)	Liters	0.473 (Imp. 0.568)
Quarts (US)	Liters	0.946 (Imp. 1.136)
Gallons (US)	Liters	3.785 (Imp. 4.546)
Ounces	Grams	28.4
Pounds	Kilograms	0.454

TO CONVERT:	TO:	MULTIPLY BY:
Millimeters	Inches	0.039
Centimeters	Inches	0.394
Meters	Feet	3.28
Meters	Yards	1.09
Square centimeters	Square inches	0.155
Square meters	Square feet	10.8
Square meters	Square yards	1.2
Milliliters	Ounces	.033
Liters	Pints (US)	2.114 (Imp. 1.76)
Liters	Quarts (US)	1.057 (Imp. 0.88)
Liters	Gallons (US)	0.264 (Imp. 0.22)
Grams	Ounces	0.035
Kilograms	Pounds	2.2

CONVERTING TEMPERATURES

Convert degrees Fahrenheit (F) to degrees Celsius (C) by following this simple formula: Subtract 32 from the Fahrenheit temperature reading. Then multiply that number by $\frac{5}{9}$. For example, 77°F - 32 = 45. 45 × $\frac{5}{9}$ = 25°C.

To convert degrees Celsius to degrees Fahrenheit, multiply the Celsius temperature reading by $\frac{9}{5}$. Then, add 32. For example, 25°C × $\frac{9}{5}$ = 45. 45 + 32 = 77°F.

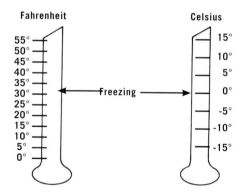

METRIC PLYWOOD PANELS

Metric plywood panels are commonly available in two sizes: 1,200 mm × 2,400 mm and 1,220 mm × 2,400 mm, which is roughly equivalent to a 4 × 8' sheet. Standard and Select sheathing panels come in standard thicknesses, while Sanded grade panels are available in special thicknesses.

STANDARD SHEATHING GRADE		SANDED GRADE	
7.5 mm	($\frac{5}{16}$")	6 mm	($\frac{4}{17}$")
9.5 mm	($\frac{3}{8}$")	8 mm	($\frac{5}{16}$")
12.5 mm	($\frac{1}{2}$")	11 mm	($\frac{7}{16}$")
15.5 mm	($\frac{5}{8}$")	14 mm	($\frac{9}{16}$")
18.5 mm	($\frac{3}{4}$")	17 mm	($\frac{2}{3}$")
20.5 mm	($\frac{13}{16}$")	19 mm	($\frac{3}{4}$")
22.5 mm	($\frac{7}{8}$")	21 mm	($\frac{13}{16}$")
25.5 mm	(1")	24 mm	($\frac{15}{16}$")

LUMBER DIMENSIONS

NOMINAL - U.S.	ACTUAL - U.S. (IN INCHES)	METRIC
1 × 2	¾ × 1½	19 × 38 mm
1 × 3	¾ × 2½	19 × 64 mm
1 × 4	¾ × 3½	19 × 89 mm
1 × 5	¾ × 4½	19 × 114 mm
1 × 6	¾ × 5½	19 × 140 mm
1 × 7	¾ × 6¼	19 × 159 mm
1 × 8	¾ × 7¼	19 × 184 mm
1 × 10	¾ × 9¼	19 × 235 mm
1 × 12	¾ × 11¼	19 × 286 mm
1¼ × 4	1 × 3½	25 × 89 mm
1¼ × 6	1 × 5½	25 × 140 mm
1¼ × 8	1 × 7¼	25 × 184 mm
1¼ × 10	1 × 9¼	25 × 235 mm
1¼ × 12	1 × 11¼	25 × 286 mm
1½ × 4	1¼ × 3½	32 × 89 mm
1½ × 6	1¼ × 5½	32 × 140 mm
1½ × 8	1¼ × 7¼	32 × 184 mm
1½ × 10	1¼ × 9¼	32 × 235 mm
1½ × 12	1¼ × 11¼	32 × 286 mm
2 × 4	1½ × 3½	38 × 89 mm
2 × 6	1½ × 5½	38 × 140 mm
2 × 8	1½ × 7¼	38 × 184 mm
2 × 10	1½ × 9¼	38 × 235 mm
2 × 12	1½ × 11¼	38 × 286 mm
3 × 6	2½ × 5½	64 × 140 mm
4 × 4	3½ × 3½	89 × 89 mm
4 × 6	3½ × 5½	89 × 140 mm

LIQUID MEASUREMENT EQUIVALENTS

1 Pint	= 16 Fluid Ounces	= 2 Cups
1 Quart	= 32 Fluid Ounces	= 2 Pints
1 Gallon	= 128 Fluid Ounces	= 4 Quarts

COUNTERBORE, SHANK & PILOT HOLE DIAMETERS

SCREW SIZE	COUNTERBORE DIAMETER FOR SCREW HEAD (IN INCHES)	CLEARANCE HOLE FOR SCREW SHANK (IN INCHES)	PILOT HOLE DIAMETER	
			HARD WOOD (IN INCHES)	SOFT WOOD (IN INCHES)
#1	.146 (9/64)	5/64	3/64	1/32
#2	1/4	3/32	3/64	1/32
#3	1/4	7/64	1/16	3/64
#4	1/4	1/8	1/16	3/64
#5	1/4	1/8	5/64	1/16
#6	5/16	9/64	3/32	5/64
#7	5/16	5/32	3/32	5/64
#8	3/8	11/64	1/8	3/32
#9	3/8	11/64	1/8	3/32
#10	3/8	3/16	1/8	7/64
#11	1/2	3/16	5/32	9/64
#12	1/2	7/32	9/64	1/8

NAILS

Nail lengths are identified by numbers from 4 to 60 followed by the letter "d," which stands for "penny." For general framing and repair work, use common or box nails. Common nails are best suited to framing work where strength is important. Box nails are smaller in diameter than common nails, which makes them easier to drive and less likely to split wood. Use box nails for light work and thin materials. Most common and box nails have a cement or vinyl coating that improves their holding power.

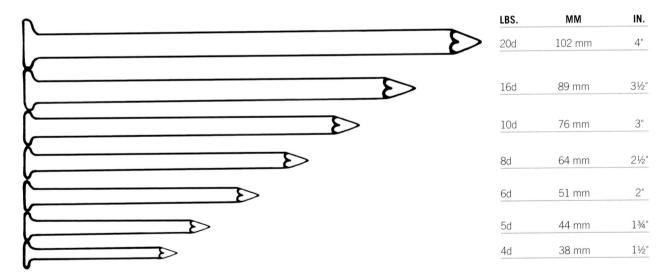

LBS.	MM	IN.
20d	102 mm	4"
16d	89 mm	3½"
10d	76 mm	3"
8d	64 mm	2½"
6d	51 mm	2"
5d	44 mm	1¾"
4d	38 mm	1½"

Index

About the Author

Bruce A. Barker is president of Dream Home Consultants, LLC., a Cary, North Carolina–based building inspection and consulting firm. He has built or inspected more than 3,000 homes during his 29 years in the construction and building inspection industries. Barker is a residential combination inspector, certified by the International Code Council. He is also a licensed contractor in Arizona, Florida, and North Carolina.

Barker is a member of the American Society of Home Inspectors (ASHI). He currently serves on the board of directors after prior service as chairman of the Society's national Standards of Practice Committee. He is also vice president of the North Carolina ASHI chapter. Barker is a frequent contributor of technical articles to ASHI Reporter, Home Energy, Builder News, and other publications. Barker is also a member of the International Code Council.

Barker graduated cum laude from the Indiana University School of Business with a degree in accounting. He also graduated from Indiana with an MBA in information systems and studied law at the Indiana University Law School. He is a member of the Beta Alpha Psi and Beta Gamma Sigma academic honor societies. Barker spent his early career as a consultant with Peat Marwick (now KPMG), an international public accounting and consulting firm, and as the owner of one of the first computer stores in the Midwest.

BLACK+DECKER THE COMPLETE GUIDE SERIES